Level 2

¡Avancemos!

Unit 4 Resource Book

HOLT McDOUGAL
a division of Houghton Mifflin Harcourt

AP and the Advanced Placement Program are registered trademarks of the College Entrance
Examination Board, which was not involved in the production of and does not endorse this product.

International Baccalaureate is a registered trademark of the International Baccalaureate Organization.

Fine Art Acknowledgments

Page 87 *Niña con bandera* (1997), Rodolfo Morales. Silkscreen, 65 cm x 50 cm. Courtesy of
Galería Arte de Oaxaca, Mexico.

Page 88 *Reina Xochtl,* Alfredo Ramos Martínez. Gouache on newspaper. Private Collection/
Bonhams, London, UK/Courtesy of Louis Stern Fine Arts, West Hollywood, CA/The Bridgeman Art
Library.

Page 89 *Mexico City* (1942), Juan O'Gorman. Tempera on masonite. Courtesy of Museo de
Arte Moderno, Mexico City, Mexico/Index/© 2005 Sandro Landucci, Mexico City/Estate of Juan
O'Gorman/The Bridgeman Art Library.

Page 90 Detail of carriages, *Plaza Mayor in Mexico* (18th century), Mexican School. Oil on canvas.
Courtesy of Museo Nacional de Historia, Mexico City, Mexico/Giraudon/The Bridgeman Art Library.

ISBN-13: 978-0-618-75358-1
ISBN-10: 0-618-75358-3   12 13 14 15 0748 18 17 16 15
Internet: www.holtmcdougal.com

4500553513

McDougal Littell

¡Avancemos!

Table of Contents

To the Teacher

Welcome to *¡Avancemos!* This exciting new Spanish program from McDougal Littell has been designed to provide you—the teacher of today's foreign language classroom—with comprehensive pedagogical support.

PRACTICE WITH A PURPOSE

Activities throughout the program begin by establishing clear goals. Look for the **¡Avanza!** arrow that uses student-friendly language to lead the way towards achievable goals. Built-in self-checks in the student text (**Para y piensa:** Did you get it?) offer the chance to assess student progress throughout the lesson. Both the student text and the workbooks offer abundant leveled practice to match varied student needs.

CULTURE AS A CORNERSTONE

¡Avancemos! celebrates the cultural diversity of the Spanish-speaking world by motivating students to think about similarities and contrasts among different Spanish-speaking cultures. Essential questions encourage thoughtful discussion and comparison between different cultures.

LANGUAGE LEARNING THAT LASTS

The program presents topics in manageable chunks that students will be able to retain and recall. "Recycle" topics are presented frequently so students don't forget material from previous lessons. Previously learned content is built upon and reinforced across the different levels of the program.

TIME-SAVING TEACHER TOOLS

Simplify your planning with McDougal Littell's exclusive teacher resources: the all-inclusive EasyPlanner DVD-ROM, ready-made Power Presentations, and the McDougal Littell Assessment System.

Unit Resource Book

Each Unit Resource Book supports a unit of *¡Avancemos!* The Unit Resource Books provide a wide variety of materials to support, practice, and expand on the material in the *¡Avancemos!* student text.

Components **Following is a list of components included in each Unit Resource Book:**

BACK TO SCHOOL RESOURCES (UNIT 1 ONLY)

Review and start-up activities to support the **Lección preliminar** of the textbook.

DID YOU GET IT? RETEACHING & PRACTICE COPYMASTERS

If students' performance on the **Para y piensa** self-check for a section does not meet your expectations, consider assigning the corresponding Did You Get It? Reteaching and Practice Copymasters. These copymasters provide extensive reteaching and additional practice for every vocabulary and grammar presentation section in *¡Avancemos!* Each vocabulary and grammar section has a corresponding three-page copymaster. The first page of the copymaster reteaches the subject material in a fresh manner. Immediately following this presentation page are two pages of practice exercises that help the student master the topic. The practice pages have engaging contexts and structures to retain students' attention.

PRACTICE GAMES

These games provide fun practice of the vocabulary and grammar just taught. They are targeted in scope so that each game practices a specific area of the **lesson**: *Práctica de vocabulario, Vocabulario en contexto, Práctica de gramática, Gramática en contexto, Todo junto, Repaso de la lección*, and the lesson's cultural information.

Video and audio resources

VIDEO ACTIVITIES

These two-page copymasters accompany the Vocabulary Video and each scene of the **Telehistoria** in Levels 1 and 2 and the **Gran desafío** in Level 3. The pre-viewing activity asks students to activate prior knowledge about a theme or subject related to the scene they will watch. The viewing activity is a simple activity for students to complete as they watch the video. The post-viewing activity gives students the opportunity to demonstrate comprehension of the video episode.

VIDEO SCRIPTS

This section provides the scripts of each video feature in the unit.

AUDIO SCRIPTS

This section contains scripts for all presentations and activities that have accompanying audio in the student text as well as in the two workbooks (*Cuaderno: práctica por niveles* and *Cuaderno para hispanohablantes*) and the assessment program.

Culture resources

MAP/CULTURE ACTIVITIES

This section contains a copymaster with geography and culture activities based on the Unit Opener in the textbook.

FINE ART ACTIVITIES

The fine art activities in every lesson ask students to analyze pieces of art that have been selected as representative of the unit location country. These copymasters can be used in conjunction with the full-color fine art transparencies in the Unit Transparency Book.

Home-school connection

FAMILY LETTERS & FAMILY INVOLVEMENT ACTIVITIES

This section is designed to help increase family support of the students' study of Spanish. The family letter keeps families abreast of the class's progress, while the family involvement activities let students share their Spanish language skills with their families in the context of a game or fun activity.

ABSENT STUDENT COPYMASTERS

The Absent Student Copymasters enable students who miss part of a **lesson** to go over the material on their own. The checkbox format allows teachers to choose and indicate exactly what material the student should complete. The Absent Student Copymasters also offer strategies and techniques to help students understand new or challenging information.

Core Ancillaries in the ¡Avancemos! Program

Leveled workbooks

CUADERNO: PRÁCTICA POR NIVELES

This core ancillary is a leveled practice workbook to supplement the student text. It is designed for use in the classroom or as homework. Students who can complete the activities correctly should be able to pass the quizzes and tests. Practice is organized into three levels of difficulty, labeled A, B, and C. Level B activities are designed to practice vocabulary, grammar, and other core concepts at a level appropriate to most of your students. Students who require more structure can complete Level A activities, while students needing more of a challenge should be encouraged to complete the activities in Level C. Each level provides a different degree of linguistic support, yet requires students to know and handle the same vocabulary and grammar content.

The following sections are included in *Cuaderno: práctica por niveles* for each **lesson**:

Vocabulario A, B, C	Escuchar A, B, C
Gramática 1 A, B, C	Leer A, B, C
Gramática 2 A, B, C	Escribir A, B, C
Integración: Hablar	Cultura A, B, C
Integración: Escribir	

CUADERNO PARA HISPANOHABLANTES

This core ancillary provides leveled practice for heritage learners of Spanish. Level A is for heritage learners who hear Spanish at home but who may speak little Spanish themselves. Level B is for those who speak some Spanish but don't read or write it yet and who may lack formal education in Spanish. Level C is for heritage learners who have had some formal schooling in Spanish. These learners can read and speak Spanish, but may need further development of their writing skills. The *Cuaderno para hispanohablantes* will ensure that heritage learners practice the same basic grammar, reading, and writing skills taught in the student text. At the same time, it offers additional instruction and challenging practice designed specifically for students with prior knowledge of Spanish.

The following sections are included in *Cuaderno para hispanohablantes* for each **lesson**:

Vocabulario A, B, C	Integración: Hablar
Vocabulario adicional	Integración: Escribir
Gramática 1 A, B, C	Lectura A, B, C
Gramática 2 A, B, C	Escritura A, B, C
Gramática adicional	Cultura A, B, C

Other Ancillaries

ASSESSMENT PROGRAM

For each level of *¡Avancemos!*, there are four complete assessment options. Every option assesses students' ability to use the lesson and unit vocabulary and grammar, as well as assessing reading, writing, listening, speaking, and cultural knowledge. The on-level tests are designed to assess the language skills of most of your students. Modified tests provide more support, explanation and scaffolding to enable students with learning difficulties to produce language at the same level as their peers. Pre-AP* tests build the test-taking skills essential to success on Advanced Placement tests. The assessments for heritage learners are all in Spanish, and take into account the strengths that native speakers bring to language learning.

In addition to leveled lesson and unit tests, there is a complete array of vocabulary, culture, and grammar quizzes. All tests include scoring rubrics and point teachers to specific resources for remediation.

UNIT TRANSPARENCY BOOKS—1 PER UNIT

Each transparency book includes:

- Map Atlas Transparencies (Unit 1 only)
- Unit Opener Map Transparencies
- Fine Art Transparencies
- Vocabulary Transparencies
- Grammar Presentation Transparencies
- Situational Transparencies with Label Overlay (plus student copymasters)
- Warm Up Transparencies
- Student Book and Workbook Answer Transparencies

LECTURAS PARA TODOS

A workbook-style reader, *Lecturas para todos*, offers all the readings from the student text as well as additional literary readings in an interactive format. In addition to the readings, they contain reading strategies, comprehension questions, and tools for developing vocabulary.

There are four sections in each *Lecturas para todos*:

- *¡Avancemos!* readings with annotated skill-building support
- *Literatura adicional*—additional literary readings
- Academic and Informational Reading Development
- Test Preparation Strategies

* AP and the Advanced Placement Program are registered trademarks of the College Entrance Examination Board, which was not involved in the production of and does not endorse this product.

LECTURAS PARA HISPANOHABLANTES

Lecturas para hispanohablantes offers additional cultural readings for heritage learners and a rich selection of literary readings. All readings supported by reading strategies, comprehension questions, tools for developing vocabulary, plus tools for literary analysis.

There are four sections in each *Lecturas para hispanohablantes*:

- *En voces* cultural readings with annotated skill-building support
- *Literatura adicional*—high-interest readings by prominent authors from around the Spanish-speaking world. Selections were chosen carefully to reflect the diversity of experiences Spanish-speakers bring to the classroom.
- Bilingual Academic and Informational Reading Development
- Bilingual Test Preparation Strategies, for success on standardized tests in English

COMIC BOOKS

These fun, motivating comic books are written in a contemporary, youthful style with full-color illustrations. Each comic uses the target language students are learning. There is one 32-page comic book for each level of the program.

TPRS: TEACHING PROFICIENCY THROUGH READING AND STORYTELLING

This book includes an up-to-date guide to TPRS and TPRS stories written by Piedad Gutiérrez that use *¡Avancemos!* lesson-specific vocabulary.

MIDDLE SCHOOL RESOURCE BOOK

- Practice activities to support the 1b Bridge lesson
- Diagnostic and Bridge Unit Tests
- Transparencies
    - Vocabulary Transparencies
    - Grammar Transparencies
    - Answer Transparencies for the Student Text
    - Bridge Warm Up Transparencies
- Audio CDs

LESSON PLANS

- Lesson Plans with suggestions for modifying instruction
- Core and Expansion options clearly noted
- IEP suggested modifications
- Substitute teacher lesson plans

BEST PRACTICES TOOLKIT

Strategies for Effective Teaching

- Research-based Learning Strategies
- Language Learning that Lasts: Teaching for Long-term Retention
- Culture as a Cornerstone/Cultural Comparisons
- English Grammar Connection
- Building Vocabulary
- Developing Reading Skills
- Differentiation
- Best Practices in Teaching Heritage Learners
- Assessment (including Portfolio Assessment, Reteaching and Remediation)
- Best Practices Swap Shop: Favorite Activities for Teaching Reading, Writing, Listening, Speaking
- Reading, Writing, Listening, and Speaking Strategies in the World Languages classroom
- ACTFL Professional Development Articles
- Thematic Teaching
- Best Practices in Middle School

Using Technology in the World Languages Classroom

Tools for Motivation

- Games in the World Languages Classroom
- Teaching Proficiency through Reading and Storytelling
- Using Comic Books for Motivation

Pre-AP and International Baccalaureate

- International Baccalaureate
- Pre-AP

Graphic Organizer Transparencies

- Teaching for Long-term Retention
- Teaching Culture
- Building Vocabulary
- Developing Reading Skills

Absent Student Copymasters—Tips for Students

LISTENING TO CDS AT HOME

- Open your text, workbook, or class notes to the corresponding pages that relate to the audio you will listen to. Read the assignment directions if there are any. Do these steps before listening to the audio selections.

- Listen to the CD in a quiet place. Play the CD loudly enough so that you can hear everything clearly. Keep focused. Play a section several times until you understand it. Listen carefully. Repeat aloud with the CD. Try to sound like the people on the CD. Stop the CD when you need to do so.

- If you are lost, stop the CD. Replay it and look at your notes. Take a break if you are not focusing. Return and continue after a break. Work in short periods of time: 5 or 10 minutes at a time so that you remain focused and energized.

QUESTION/ANSWER SELECTIONS

- If there is a question/answer selection, read the question aloud several times. Write down the question. Highlight the key words, verb endings, and any new words. Look up new words and write their meaning. Then say everything aloud.

- One useful strategy for figuring out questions is to put parentheses around groups of words that go together. For example: **(¿Cuántos niños)(van)(al estadio)(a las tres?)** Read each group of words one at a time. Check for meaning. Write out answers. Highlight key words and verb endings. Say the question aloud. Read the answer aloud. Ask yourself if you wrote what you meant.

- Be sure to say everything aloud several times before moving on to the next question. Check for spelling, verb endings, and accent marks.

FLASHCARDS FOR VOCABULARY

- If you have Internet access, go to ClassZone at classzone.com. All the vocabulary taught in *¡Avancemos!* is available on electronic flashcards. Look for the flashcards in the *¡Avancemos!* section of ClassZone.

- If you don't have Internet access, write the Spanish word or phrase on one side of a 3″× 5″ card, and the English translation on the other side. Illustrate your flashcards when possible. Be sure to highlight any verb endings, accent marks, or other special spellings that will need a bit of extra attention.

GRAMMAR ACTIVITIES

- Underline or highlight all verb endings and adjective agreements. For example:
  Nosotros com<u>emos</u> pollo ric<u>o</u>.

- Underline or highlight infinitive endings: **trabaj<u>ar</u>**.

- Underline or highlight accented letters. Say aloud and be louder on the accented letters. Listen carefully for the loudness. This will remind you where to write your accent mark. For example: **l<u>á</u>piz, l<u>á</u>pices, <u>á</u>rbol, <u>á</u>rboles**

- When writing a sentence, be sure to ask yourself, "What do I mean? What am I trying to say?" Then check your sentence to be sure that you wrote what you wanted to say.

- Mark patterns with a highlighter. For example, for stem-changing verbs, you can draw a "boot" around the letters that change:

v**ue**lvo	volvemos
v**ue**lves	volvéis
v**ue**lve	v**ue**lven

READING AND CULTURE SECTIONS

- Read the strategy box. Copy the graphic organizer so you can fill it out as you read.

- Look at the title and subtitles before you begin to read. Then look at and study any photos and read the captions. Translate the captions only if you can't understand them at all. Before you begin to read, guess what the selection will be about. What do you think that you will learn? What do you already know about this topic?

- Read any comprehension questions before beginning to read the paragraphs. This will help you focus on the upcoming reading selection. Copy the questions and highlight key words.

- Reread one or two of the questions and then go to the text. Begin to read the selection carefully. Read it again. On a sticky note, write down the appropriate question number next to where the answer lies in the text. This will help you keep track of what the questions have asked you and will help you focus when you go back to reread it later, perhaps in preparation for a quiz or test.

- Highlight any new words. Make a list or flashcards of new words. Look up their meanings. Study them. Quiz yourself or have a partner quiz you. Then go back to the comprehension questions and check your answers from memory. Look back at the text if you need to verify your answers.

PAIRED PRACTICE EXERCISES

- If there is an exercise for partners, practice both parts at home.
- If no partner is available, write out both scripts and practice both roles aloud. Highlight and underline key words, verb endings, and accent marks.

WRITING PROJECTS

- Brainstorm ideas before writing.
- Make lists of your ideas.
- Put numbers next to the ideas to determine the order in which you want to write about them.
- Group your ideas into paragraphs.
- Skip lines in your rough draft.
- Have a partner read your work and give you feedback on the meaning and language structure.
- Set it aside and reread it at least once before doing a final draft. Double-check verb endings, adjective agreements, and accents.
- Read it once again to check that you said what you meant to say.
- Be sure to have a title and any necessary illustrations or bibliography.

Did You Get It? *Presentación de vocabulario*

> **¡AVANZA!**   **Goal:**   Learn the words about legends and stories.

Writing a Legend

Do you enjoy reading legends? Have you ever written a legend? Read the following tips to learn ways to tell a legend, or **contar una leyenda,** in Spanish.

Legends often start with traditional phrases. In English "Once upon a time..." is a phrase that you probably have read or heard. To start a legend in Spanish you can use:

Había una vez...   *Once upon a time there was / were...*

Hace muchos siglos...   *Many centuries ago...*

Legends also have main characters that can be people, animals, gods or imaginary creatures. Here are some characters, or **personajes,** you can use in your legend.

Los personajes

el (la) dios(a) *(god goddess)*   **el héroe** *(hero)*

el ejército *(army)*   **la heroína** *(heroine)*

el emperador *(emperor)*   **el (la) joven** *(young man/woman)*

el enemigo *(enemy)*   **la princesa** *(princess)*

el guerrero *(warrior)*   **el/la querido(a)** *(beloved (adj.))*

hermoso(a) *(handsome; pretty)*   **valiente** *(brave)*

Once you have your characters, you need to create a setting for your legend. Here are some Spanish words for places you could use:

la montaña *(mountain)*   **el palacio** *(palace)*   **el volcán** *(volcano)*

Now that your legend has characters and a place, you need to add some action. Here are some events that could happen in the legend and some action words to talk about what your characters do.

estar enamorado(a) (de) *(to be in love (with))*

la batalla *(battle)*   **tener celos** *(to be jealous)*   **la guerra** *(war)*

casarse *(to get married)*   **morir (ue)** *(to die)*   **pelear** *(to fight)*

llevar *(to take; to carry)*   **regresar** *(to return)*   **llorar** *(to cry)*

Every good legend ends with a moral or lesson. Use these words to say what your legend is about or to describe the moral or your story.

la narración *narration*   **histórico(a)** *(historic; historical)*

el mensaje *lesson / moral of the story*

sobre *about*

Did You Get It? *Práctica de vocabulario*

> **¡AVANZA!** **Goal:** Learn the words about legends and stories.

❶ Circle the word that doesn't belong in each group.

1. heroína   héroe   enemigo

2. guerrero   mensaje   valiente

3. jóvenes   batallas   personajes

4. volcán   narración   leyenda

5. guerra   princesa   hermosa

6. ejército   batalla   azteca

❷ Which word corresponds to each description?

1. A large group of soldiers who battle in the name of a king or emperor.
   batalla   emperador   ejército

2. The daughter of a king or queen.
   diosa   princesa   heroína

3. To have tears coming out of your eyes.
   llevar   llorar   pelear

4. The bad guy in a story, or the person who's against the hero.
   enemigo   enamorado   héroe

5. The description of a man who can think only of his true love.
   enamorado   enemigo   hermoso

6. A very brave person who is not afraid of anything.
   hermosa   valiente   guerrero

❸ Based on what you have learned about legends, decide whether each sentence is true (T) or false (F).

1. A legend also can be called a **narración histórica**. T F
2. The good guy in a legend is usually **el héroe**. T F
3. **El enemigo** is portrayed as a nice guy. T F
4. **Un palacio** is usually a small, modest building. T F
5. Often the princess and the hero **están enamorados**. T F
6. The characters in the story are **los personajes**. T F

❹ Choose a word or phrase from the box to complete the following sentences.

celos	batalla	enemigo	princesa	emperador	hermosa
leyenda	enamorada	guerrero	se casan	valiente	ejército

Una **1.** _____ azteca

Una **2.** _____ vive en un gran palacio con su padre, el

3. _____ azteca. La princesa es **4.** _____ . Ella está

5. _____ de un **6.** _____ . El querido es

7. _____ . Es el más valiente del **8.** _____ . Hay un

9. _____ y él tiene **10.** _____ de los dos porque él

también está enamorado de la princesa. El guerrero valiente lucha en una

11. _____ contra el enemigo. El enemigo muere. Entonces la princesa

y el guerrero valiente **12.** _____ .

❺ Complete a description of these people or things below using the appropriate past participle of the verb in parentheses.

1. una princesa _____ (cansar)

2. un emperador _____ (casar)

3. una puerta _____ (cerrar)

4. unos guerreros _____ (entrenar)

5. un palacio _____ (transformar)

6. unas batallas _____ (ganar)

7. unos dioses _____ (enojar)

8. un enemigo _____ (perder)

Did You Get It? *Presentación de gramática*

UNIDAD 4 Lección 1

Reteaching and Practice

| ¡AVANZA! | **Goal:** Learn how to form and use the imperfect tense. |

The Imperfect Tense

- **Regular Verbs**
  Study the following three verbs in the imperfect tense.

-ar verbs: cantar – *to sing*	-er verbs: tener – *to have*	-ir verbs: vivir – *to live*
yo cant**aba**	yo ten**ía**	yo viv**ía**
tú cant**abas**	tú ten**ías**	tú viv**ías**
usted cant**aba**	usted ten**ía**	usted viv**ía**
él/ella cant**aba**	él/ella ten**ía**	él/ella viv**ía**
nosotros(as) cant**ábamos**	nosotros(as) ten**íamos**	nosotros(as) viv**íamos**
vosostros(as) cant**abais**	vosotros(as) ten**íais**	vosotros(as) viv**íais**
ustedes cantab**an**	ustedes ten**ían**	ustedes viv**ían**
ellos/ellas cant**aban**	ellos/ellas ten**ían**	ellos/ellas viv**ían**

EXPLANATION: To talk about what you used to do, use the imperfect tense. For example, **yo cantaba** means *I used to sing* or *I was singing*. All **-ar** verbs are regular in the imperfect tense. The **-er** verbs and **-ir** verbs have the same endings. Notice that the first-person plural of all verbs in the imperfect has an accent.

- **Irregular Verbs**
  Study the forms of these verbs in the imperfect tense.

ir – *to go*	ser – *to be*	ver – *to see*
yo **iba**	yo **era**	yo **veía**
tú **ibas**	tú **eras**	tú **veías**
usted **iba**	usted **era**	usted **veía**
él/ella **iba**	él/ella **era**	él/ella **veía**
nosotros(as) **íbamos**	nosotros(as) **éramos**	nosotros(as) **veíamos**
vosostros(as) **ibais**	vosostros(as) **erais**	vosostros(as) **veíais**
ellos/ellas **iban**	ellos/ellas **eran**	ellos/ellas **veían**

EXPLANATION: Only three verbs in Spanish are irregular in the imperfect tense: **ir**, **ser**, and **ver**.

Did You Get It? *Práctica de gramática*

> **¡AVANZA!**   **Goal:**   Learn how to form and use the imperfect tense.

1 Write the correct form of each regular verb in the imperfect tense.

1. yo _____ (estar)

2. ellos _____ (cantar)

3. él _____ (escribir)

4. nosotros _____ (hacer)

5. Anita _____ (salir)

6. tú _____ (tener)

7. los chicos _____ (estudiar)

8. ustedes _____ (jugar)

9. vosotros _____ (comer)

10. Rodrigo y yo _____ (vivir)

2 Write the correct form of the boldfaced verb in the imperfect tense based on the subject.

1. **Vemos** a los chicos.

   a. yo _____

   b. él _____

   c. vosotras _____

   d. mi amigo y yo _____

   e. ellos _____

2. **Voy** a la tienda.

   a. tú _____

   b. usted _____

   c. los amigos _____

   d. el maestro de francés _____

   e. ustedes _____

3. **Son** simpáticos.

   a. ellas _____

   b. yo _____

   c. tus padres _____

   d. tú _____

   e. vosotros _____

❸ Change each verb to the imperfect tense. Follow the model.

Modelo: María <u>ve</u> la televisión.

María *veía* la televisión.

1. Roberto <u>juega</u> al fútbol. / Roberto _____ al fútbol.

2. Mi hermana y yo <u>hacemos</u> la tarea. / Mi hermana y yo _____ la tarea.

3. Mis amigos y yo <u>vemos</u> el video. / Mis amigos y yo _____ el video.

4. Pablito y Lucila <u>lloran</u> mucho. / Pablito y Lucila _____ mucho.

5. José Antonio <u>es</u> joven. / José Antonio _____ joven.

6. Nosotros <u>vamos</u> al parque. / Nosotros _____ al parque.

7. Ustedes <u>ven</u> el programa. / Ustedes _____ el programa.

8. Tú <u>sales</u> mucho. / Tú _____ mucho.

9. Yo <u>practico</u> deportes. / Yo _____ deportes.

10. La maestra de español <u>enseña</u> bien. / La maestra de español _____ bien.

❹ Choose a word from the box to complete Marco's letter.

iba	venía	trabajaban	trabajaba	caminábamos
era	íbamos	hacíamos	veíamos	dormíamos
vivía	hacía	cenábamos	jugábamos	tenía

Te voy a contar cómo **1.** _____ mi vida cuando yo

2. _____ quince años y **3.** _____ en tu ciudad.

Todos los días, yo **4.** _____ a la escuela por la mañana.

Después de las clases, mi mamá **5.** _____ a la escuela y ella y yo

6. _____ hasta su oficina. Allí, mi tía y ella **7.** _____

un rato y mi primo y yo **8.** _____ la tarea. Por la tarde, mis amigos

y yo **9.** _____ juntos en el parque o **10.** _____ una

película en mi casa. Después, todos nosotros **11.** _____ y nos

12. _____ antes de las diez.

❺ Write a sentence describing two things you used to do when you were young.

Cuando yo era niño(a), _____

_____

Did You Get It? *Presentación de gramática*

| ¡AVANZA! | **Goal:** | Learn the differences between the preterite and imperfect tenses. Then use both to narrate past events. |

Preterite vs. Imperfect

Read the sentences below, paying attention to the highlighted verbs. The ones on the left are in the imperfect tense and the ones on the right are in the preterite tense.

Imperfect	**Preterite**
Carlos **iba** a España cada año.	El año pasado Carlos **fue** a México.
*(Carlos **used to go** to Spain every year.)*	*(Last year, Carlos **went** to Mexico.)*
Antes, la clase **empezaba** a la una.	Ayer la clase **empezó** a la una.
*(Before, class **used to start** at 8 o'clock.)*	*(Yesterday, class **started** at 8 o'clock.)*

Yo **veía** la televisión cuando mis amigos **llegaron**.
*(I **was watching** TV when my friends **arrived**.)*

Felipe **hacía** la tarea cuando su mamá lo **llamó** para comer.
*(Felipe **was doing** homework when his mother **called** him to eat.)*

EXPLANATION: Think about all actions as having a beginning, a middle, and an end.

• If you talk about the middle of a continuing action, you use the **imperfect** tense. For example:

Last night, I **was studying** Spanish when the phone rang.
*(Anoche, **estudiaba** español cuando el teléfono sonó.)*

I **used to go** to the park when I was young.
*(Yo **iba** al parque cuando era joven.)*

• If you talk about the beginning or the end of an action, you use the **preterite** tense. For example:

Last night I **studied** Spanish.
*(Anoche **estudié** español)*

I **went** to the park at 3 o'clock.
*(**Fui** al parque a las tres.)*

Did You Get It? *Práctica de gramática*

¡AVANZA!	**Goal:**	Learn the differences between the preterite and imperfect tenses. Then use both to narrate past events.

❶ Read the following sentences and decide whether the underlined verbs would be in the preterite (P) or imperfect (I) tense.

1. In 1995 my family and I <u>moved</u> across the country.   P   I

2. When my dad <u>got</u> his new job, we <u>became</u> very rich.   P   I

3. Back then, my sister <u>used to spend</u> the summer with my aunt.   P   I

4. One summer, I <u>went</u> to Ireland with my family.   P   I

5. My grandfather <u>used to visit</u> us every afternoon in our new home.   P   I

6. Then, in 1996, my brother Joe <u>was born</u>.   P   I

7. I <u>went</u> to the hospital to see him the next day.   P   I

8. After that, Joe and I <u>would spend</u> every afternoon together.   P   I

❷ Choose the correct translation.

1. Ellos llegaron tarde a la fiesta.
   a. They arrived to the party late.
   b. They were arriving to the party late.

2. Usted iba de vacaciones a Perú.
   a. You went on vacation to Peru.
   b. You used to go on vacation to Peru.

3. Nosotros caminamos a la tienda con Elisa y Lupe.
   a. We walked to the store with Elisa and Lupe.
   b. We were walking to the store with Elisa and Lupe.

4. Yo hacía mi tarea en la tarde.
   a. I did my homework in the afternoon.
   b. I used to do my homework in the afternoon.

5. Empezaba a llover cuando salí de la casa.
   a. It started to rain when I was leaving the house.
   b. It was starting to rain when I left the house.

6. Veíamos la televisión cuando los abuelos llegaron.
   a. We watched TV when our grandparents arrived.
   b. We were watching TV when our grandparents arrived.

❸ Preterite or Imperfect? Complete the e-mail by circling the appropriate verb.

Alberto:

Tengo que contarte algo importante. El fin de semana pasado, mis amigas
y yo **1.** (fuimos / íbamos) a una fiesta. Yo **2.** (estaba / estuve) muy
nerviosa porque la fiesta **3.** (fue / era) en casa de mi peor enemiga, pero
todo **4.** (fue / iba) muy bien. **5.** (Llegábamos / Llegamos) allí a las
cinco de la tarde y mi enemiga **6.** (llevaba / llevó) un vestido horrible.
Mis amigas y yo **7.** (jugábamos / jugamos) en el jardín un rato pero
después **8.** (empezó / empezaba) a llover. Más tarde, **9.** (llegó / llegaba)
el papá de mi amiga y nos **10.** (regaló / regalaba) recuerdos a todos. La
verdad es que **11.** (fue / era) una tarde muy especial y mis amigas y yo
lo **12.** (pasábamos / pasamos) muy bien. Bueno, espero verte pronto.

Cristina

❹ Preterite or Imperfect? Complete the sentences with the correct form of the verb.

1. Cuando yo _____ pequeña, mi mamá tenía muchas películas en casa. (**ser**)

2. A mi mamá sólo le _____ ver películas de amor. (**gustar**)

3. Yo _____ ver historias de príncipes y princesas. (**preferir**)

4. Un día mi papá _____ a casa con una película de guerra. (**llegar**)

5. Mi hermano Julio _____ contento. (**estar**)

6. Él siempre _____ ver películas de acción o de guerra. (**querer**)

7. Esa noche, Julio, papá y yo _____ la película. (**ver**)

❺ Use the words given to translate the following sentences.

1. Yesterday I ate French fries.   ayer / comer / papas fritas

_____

2. Last year I went to Mexico.   el año pasado / ir / a Mexico.

_____

3. When I was young, I used to ride my bicycle.   cuando / ser / joven / montar en
bicicleta

_____

4. They were studying when the pizza arrived.   estudiar / cuando / la pizza / llegar

_____

5. When we lived in Boston, we used to go to the park every day.
cuando / vivir / en Boston / ir / al parque / todos los días

_____

¿Recuerdas?

Expressions of Frequency

- Study the following expressions of frequency.

    nunca *(never)*

    de vez en cuando *(once in a while)*

    generalmente *(generally)*

    mucho *(a lot)*

    muchas veces *(often, many times)*

    a veces *(sometimes)*

    todos los días *(every day)*

    siempre *(always)*

    frecuentemente *(frequently)*

EXPLANATION: These expressions help you talk about how often you do or did things.

Práctica

Answer the questions using an expression of frequency to say how often you and others did the following things when you were a child.

1. ¿Ibas a jugar a casa de tus amigos? _____

2. ¿Iban a la playa tú y tu familia? _____

3. ¿Visitabas Argentina? _____

4. ¿Tu abuela preparaba comidas muy ricas para cenar? _____

5. ¿Leías libros en español? _____

6. ¿Veían películas tus amigos y tú? _____

7. ¿Andabas en patineta con tus amigos? _____

8. ¿Montabas en bicicleta con tus padres? _____

Level 2 p. 207

♻ ¿Recuerdas?

Weather Expressions

- Study the names of the seasons in Spanish.

  la primavera *(spring)*   **el verano** *(summer)*

  el otoño *(fall)*   **el invierno** *(winter)*

- Now study the following weather expressions in Spanish.

  ¿Que tiempo hace? *(What is the weather like?)*

  Hace frío. *(It is cold.)*   **Hace calor.** *(It is hot.)*

  Hace sol. *(It is sunny.)*   **Llueve.** *(It is raining.)*

  Hace viento. *(It is windy.)*   **Nieva.** *(It is snowing.)*

EXPLANATION: All weather expressions take the third-person singular of the verb. These are considered impersonal sentences in Spanish.

Práctica

❶ Look at the weather expressions above and select one that usually goes with each of the seasons.

La primavera: _____

El verano: _____

El otoño: _____

El invierno: _____

❷ Now use your own experience to answer these questions about your activities in different types of weather.

1. ¿Qué te gusta hacer cuando hace mucho calor?

_____

2. ¿Qué haces generalmente cuando hace mucho frío?

_____

3. Normalmente, ¿qué tiempo hace en tu ciudad en el mes de julio?

_____

4. ¿Qué te gusta hacer cuando nieva? ¿Adónde te gusta ir?

_____

5. ¿Cuál es tu estación favorita? ¿Por qué?

_____

♻ ¿Recuerdas?

Daily Activities

- Study the list of daily activities below.

alquilar un DVD *(to rent a DVD)*   **beber** *(to drink)*

comprar *(to buy)*   **comer** *(to eat)*

correr *(to run)*   **estudiar español** *(to study Spanish)*

descansar *(to rest)*   **dibujar** *(to draw)*

escuchar música *(to listen to music)*   **trabajar** *(to work)*

hablar por teléfono *(to talk on the phone)*   **hacer la tarea** *(to do homework)*

leer un libro *(to read a book)*   **mirar la televisión** *(to watch TV)*

montar en bicicleta *(to ride a bike)*   **pasear** *(to take a walk)*

practicar deportes *(to practice sports)*   **jugar al fútbol** *(to play soccer)*

tocar la guitarra *(to play guitar)*

escribir correos electrónicos *(to write e-mails)*

Práctica

Complete the following sentences to state some of the things you did habitually last year. Remember that habitual actions take the imperfect tense.

1. Todos los días, después de clase, _____

2. Los sábados por la mañana, _____

3. Los domingos, a mi familia y a mí nos gustaba _____

4. Algunas veces, cuando hacía buen tiempo, _____

5. Cuando hacía mal tiempo, no me gustaba _____

6. Cuando no teníamos tarea, a mis amigos y a mí _____

7. Cuando llovía, _____

8. En mi tiempo libre, yo siempre _____

Did You Get It? *Presentación de vocabulario*

| ¡AVANZA! | **Goal:** | Learn words to discuss early civilizations and modern cities. Then use what you have learned to talk about cities, both ancient and modern. |

Early and Modern Civilizations

- In many cities around the globe, you can view a mix of two worlds, the old and the new. Study the words and expressions about these two worlds below.

Civilizaciones antiguas

antiguo(a) *ancient; (old)*   **la civilización** *(civilization)*

las ruinas *(ruins)*   **el templo** *(temple)*

la pirámide *(pyramid)*   **la tumba** *(tomb)*

la excavación *(excavation)*   **la religión** *(religion)*

la agricultura *(agriculture)*   **el objeto** *(object)*

el (la) agricultor *(farmer)*   **el calendario azteca** *(Aztec calendar)*

la herramienta *(tool)*   **los toltecas** *(Toltecs)*

el monumento *(monument)*   **cazar** *(to hunt)*

la estatua *(statue)*   **construir** *(to build)*

Ciudades modernas

el rascacielos *(skyscraper)*   **la acera** *(sidewalk)*

la catedral *(cathedral)*   **la cuadra** *(city block)*

el semáforo *(traffic light)*   **la esquina** *(corner)*

el barrio *(neighborhood)*   **el edificio** *(building)*

la plaza *(square)*   **avanzado(a)** *(advanced)*

la avenida *(avenue)*   **moderno(a)** *(modern)*

- Now, if someone wants to ask you how to get to a certain place, they will ask: **¿Cómo llego a...?** *(How do I get to...?)*. You can use the words and expressions below to give them directions.

doblar a la derecha *(to turn right)*   **entre** *(between)*

doblar a la izquierda *(to turn left)*   **frente a** *(across from, facing)*

seguir derecho *(to go straight)*   **desde** *(from)*

cruzar *(to cross)*   **hasta** *(to, until)*

Did You Get It? *Práctica de vocabulario*

> **¡AVANZA!** **Goal:** Learn words to discuss early civilizations and modern cities. Then use what you have learned to talk about cities, both ancient and modern.

❶ Match each picture with the word or phrase that describes it.

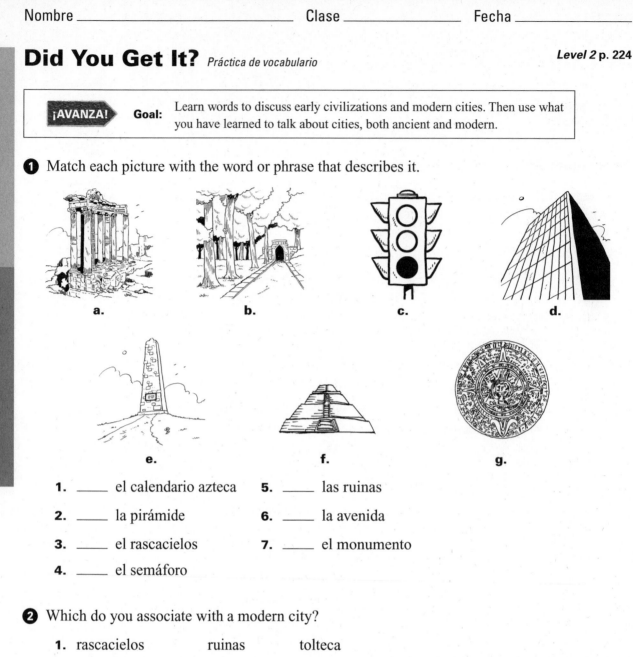

a.   b.   c.   d.

e.   f.   g.

1. ____ el calendario azteca   **5.** ____ las ruinas

2. ____ la pirámide   **6.** ____ la avenida

3. ____ el rascacielos   **7.** ____ el monumento

4. ____ el semáforo

❷ Which do you associate with a modern city?

1. rascacielos   ruinas   tolteca

2. excavación   antigua   acera

3. pirámide   agricultura   semáforo

4. calendario azteca   barrio   religiones antiguas

5. edificio   pirámide   ruinas

3 Decide whether each sentence describes an ancient area of a city (A) or a modern area (M).

1. Esta área tiene muchas ruinas y objetos de otras civilizaciones.   A   M
2. Me gustan mucho las avenidas llenas de tiendas y de gente.   A   M
3. A veces paseo cerca de las excavaciones.   A   M
4. En mi barrio, hay muchos rascacielos y monumentos.   A   M
5. La catedral está cerca del templo azteca.   A   M
6. En todas las plazas hay uno o dos semáforos.   A   M
7. Los habitantes del lugar practicaban la agricultura y cazaban animales.   A   M

4 Complete each sentence with a word from the box.

barrio	agricultura	edificio	semáforos	catedral
calendario	avenida	monumentos	cazaban	templos

1. En la ciudad hay _____ en todas las calles.
2. Los aztecas usaban un _____ especial.
3. Los coches corren mucho en la _____ .
4. En México hay muchos _____ para los dioses antiguos.
5. Hay muchos _____ en Washington, D.C.
6. Los pueblos antiguos _____ animales para comer.
7. Los domingos voy a la _____ con mi familia.
8. Los pueblos antiguos practicaban la _____ .
9. Mi padre trabaja en el _____ más alto y nuevo del centro.
10. Yo vivo en una casa nueva que está en un _____ muy moderno.

5 Complete the following description of your city, using the new vocabulary about old and modern cities.

Mi ciudad es **1.** _____ . En mi ciudad hay **2.** _____ , pero no hay **3.** _____ . Las plazas de mi ciudad son **4.** _____ y en las avenidas hay **5.** _____ . El monumento que más me gusta de mi ciudad es **6.** _____ . Mi estatua favorita está en **7.** _____ .

Did You Get It? *Presentación de gramática*

Level 2 p. 227

 **¡AVANZA!** **Goal:** Learn the spelling changes of **-car**, **-gar**, and **-zar** verbs in the preterite. Then use these verbs to talk about what you did.

Preterite of *-car*, *-gar*, and *-zar* Verbs

Read the following questions and answers, paying special attention to the highlighted verbs.

¿**Buscaste** las ruinas antiguas?	*(Did you look for the old ruins?)*
Sí, las **busqué** en un mapa de México.	*(Yes, I looked for them on a map of Mexico.)*
José también las **buscó.**	*(José looked for them, too.)*
¿**Pagaste** los boletos para visitar las ruinas?	*(Did you pay for the tickets to visit the ruins?)*
No, no los **pagué.**	*(No, I didn't pay for them.)*
No importa. Andrea los **pagó.**	*(It doesn't matter. Andrea paid for them.)*
¿**Empezaste** un diario sobre las ruinas antiguas?	*(Did you start a journal about the old ruins?)*
Sí, **empecé** uno la semana pasada.	*(Yes, I started one last week.)*
Luis **empezó** uno también.	*(Luis started one, too.)*

EXPLANATION: The stems of the verbs **buscar**, **pagar**, and **empezar** change in the first-person singular of the preterite tense. Note that the **c** in **buscar** changes to **qu**, the **g** in **pagar** changes to **gu** and the **z** in **empezar** changes to **c**. This happens only in the first-person singular and applies to other verbs ending in **-car**, **-gar**, and **-zar**. Look at the following list. How many of these verbs do you already know?

sacar	⟶	yo sa**qué**
tocar	⟶	yo to**qué**
llegar	⟶	yo lle**gué**
jugar	⟶	yo ju**gué**
almorzar	⟶	yo almor**cé**
comenzar	⟶	yo comen**cé**

Did You Get It? *Práctica de gramática*

> ¡AVANZA!   **Goal:** Learn the spelling changes of **-car**, **-gar**, and **-zar** verbs in the preterite. Then use these verbs to say what you did.

1 Change the boldfaced verb from the present tense to the preterite tense.

1. Yo **cruzo** la calle.

   1. yo _____
   2. ella _____
   3. nosotros _____
   4. tú _____
   5. los chicos _____

2. Mi madre **paga** la cuenta.

   1. tú _____
   2. mi amigos y yo _____
   3. él _____
   4. Ana y Felipe _____
   5. yo _____

3. Alisa **saca** buenas notas.

   1. nosotras _____
   2. yo _____
   3. ellas _____
   4. vosotros _____
   5. usted _____

2 Answer the questions, using the model as a guide.

Modelo: ¿Llegaste a México por la mañana?   *Sí, llegué a México por la mañana.*

1. ¿Comenzaste tu visita a México en autobús?

   _____

2. ¿Sacaste un boleto de autobús para varios días?

   _____

3. ¿Pagaste mucho dinero para entrar a ver las ruinas?

   _____

4. ¿Almorzaste en algún sitio típico mexicano?

   _____

5. ¿Tocaste algún monumento azteca durante tu visita?

   _____

6. ¿Buscaste algún lugar especial para pasar la tarde?

   _____

❸ Complete each sentence in the preterite tense, using an appropriate verb from the box. Do not use any verb more than once.

buscar	apagar	tocar	organizar	leer
practicar	empezar	almorzar	llegar	construir

1. Ayer me levanté y antes de ir a la escuela _____ mis libros.

2. Después de vestirme y desayunar, _____ a caminar hacia la escuela.

3. Quince minutos más tarde _____ a la escuela.

4. En la clase de historia la profesora nos _____ una leyenda muy interesante sobre los dioses aztecas.

5. A las doce, _____ sopa de tomate con mi hermano.

6. En la clase de estudios sociales, aprendimos sobre los toltecas y cómo ellos _____ las pirámides de Tula.

7. Por la tarde, después de mis clases, yo _____ deportes.

8. A las seis de la tarde, yo _____ la guitarra un rato.

9. Por la noche, antes de acostarme, _____ mis cosas.

10. Finalmente, antes de dormirme, yo _____ la luz de mi cuarto.

❹ Choose words from the box to write three sentences about what you did the last time you visited a new town or city.

buscar	pagar	llegar	comprar	sacar	comenzar
empezar	practicar	cruzar	almorzar	apagar	

1. _____

2. _____

3. _____

Did You Get It? *Presentación de gramática*

| ¡AVANZA! | **Goal:** Learn more irregular preterite stems and endings. |

More Verbs with Irregular Preterite Stems

- Other Spanish verbs are irregular in the preterite tense. Study the conjugations of these two verbs.

venir *(to come)*	querer *(to want)*
yo v**ine**	yo qu**ise**
tú v**iniste**	tú qu**isiste**
usted/él/ella v**ino**	usted/él/ella qu**iso**
nosotros(as) v**inimos**	nosotros(as) qu**isimos**
vosotros(as) v**inisteis**	vosotros(as) qu**isisteis**
ustedes/ellos(as) v**inieron**	ustedes/ellos(as) qu**isieron**

EXPLANATION: In **venir** and **querer** the stem **e** changes to an **i** in the preterite tense. The endings for the irregular verbs are are **-e**, **-iste**, **-o**, **-imos**, **-isteis**, and **-ieron**.

- Now study these verbs.

decir *(to say)*	traducir *(to translate)*	traer *(to bring)*
yo di**je**	yo tradu**je**	yo tra**je**
tú di**jiste**	tú tradu**jiste**	tú tra**jiste**
usted/él/ella di**jo**	usted/él/ella tradu**jo**	usted/él/ella tra**jo**
nosotros(as) di**jimos**	nosotros(as) tradu**jimos**	nosotros(as) tra**jimos**
vosotros(as) di**jisteis**	vosotros(as) tradu**jisteis**	vosotros(as) tra**jisteis**
ustedes/ellos(as) di**jeron**	ustedes/ellos(as) tradu**jeron**	ustedes/ellos(as) tra**jeron**

EXPLANATION: The stem in verbs that end in **-cir**, such as **decir** or **traducir**, change to **j**. **Traer** also has **j** in its stem. Note that the third-person plural ending in these three verbs is **-eron**.

Did You Get It? *Práctica de gramática*

Level 2 pp. 233–234

> **¡AVANZA!** **Goal:** Learn more irregular preterite stems and endings.

1 Choose the correct verb.

1. Cuando fuimos de viaje, mis padres y yo _____ tomar muchas fotos.
   a. quisieron **b.** quise **c.** quisimos

2. Mi hermana y mi prima también _____ con nosotros en el viaje.
   a. vino **b.** vinieron **c.** viniste

3. El guía _____ que no podíamos tomar fotos de las ruinas.
   a. dijo **b.** dijeron **c.** dije

4. Nosotros también _____ un video del viaje.
   a. trajimos **b.** trajeron **c.** trajiste

5. Mi amigo Beto también _____ venir con nosotros.
   a. quisieron **b.** quiso **c.** quise

6. Mis padres _____ que fue el mejor viaje de su vida.
   a. dije **b.** dijo **c.** dijeron

2 Use the verb **traer** and follow the model to explain what the following people brought to the History of Mexico festival.

Modelo: María y Fernando / postales de la Península de Yucatán.
   María y Fernando trajeron postales de la Península de Yucatán.

1. José / fotos / ruinas toltecas

   _____

2. Marta y Andrea / collar azteca

   _____

3. Yo / calendario mexicano / muy antiguo

   _____

4. Mi hermana y yo / objetos / excavaciones en México

   _____

5. Tú / una escultura mexicana / muy linda

   _____

3 Complete the postcard by writing all verbs in the correct preterite form.

Hola, Juanita:

¿Sabías que el mes pasado fui a México con mi familia? Primero, nosotros **1.** _____ **(tomar)** un avión hasta la Ciudad de México. Cuando llegamos a la primera excavación mi papá **2.** _____ **(querer)** tomar algunas fotos, pero el guía de la excursión **3.** _____ **(decir)** que no estaba permitido usar la cámara. Cuando volvimos del viaje, yo **4.** _____ **(traer)** unas postales para mis amigos y mis padres **5.** _____ **(traer)** artesanías para mis abuelos. Nosotros **6.** _____ **(venir)** a casa muy cansados.

Sonia

4 Think about the last field trip you took with your classmates and answer the questions.

1. ¿Quienes quisieron ir a la excursión?

_____

2. ¿Hubo estudiantes que quisieron ir a la excursión pero no pudieron?

_____

3. ¿Buscaste algún objeto interesante mientras estabas en la excursión?

_____

4. ¿Qué fue lo más interesante que trajeron los otros estudiantes?

_____

5. ¿Qué dijo tu profesor o profesora después de la excursión?

_____

♻ ¿Recuerdas?

Daily Activities

- Study the following list of daily activities. Then place an X next to all the activities in the list that you did yesterday.

estudié *(I studied)*

cociné *(I cooked)*

descansé *(I rested)*

dibujé *(I drew)*

paseé *(I took a walk)*

hice la tarea *(I did homework)*

jugué al fútbol *(I played soccer)*

toqué el piano *(I played piano)*

miré la televisión *(I watched TV)*

fui de compras *(I went shopping)*

monté en bicicleta *(I rode a bike)*

escribí correos electrónicos *(I wrote e-mails)*

escuché música *(I listened to music)*

hablé por teléfono *(I talked on the phone)*

practiqué deportes *(I practiced sports)*

Práctica

Answer the following questions in complete sentences, using expressions from the list above.

1. ¿Qué hiciste el día de tu cumpleaños el año pasado?

   _____

2. ¿Qué es lo primero que hiciste después de desayunar ayer?

   _____

3. ¿Qué actividades hiciste después de la escuela el miércoles pasado?

   _____

4. ¿Cuándo hablaste por teléfono por última vez?

   _____

5. ¿A quién le escribiste el último correo electrónico?

   _____

6. ¿Cuándo fue la última vez que montaste en bicicleta?

   _____

7. ¿Adónde paseaste con tus amigos o familia el fin de semana pasado?

   _____

8. ¿Adónde fuiste la última vez que practicaste deportes?

   _____

✾ ¿Recuerdas?

Arts and Crafts

• Study the following words and expressions about arts and crafts.

    las joyas *(jewelry)*
    el arete *(earring)*
    el anillo *(ring)*
    el collar *(necklace)*

    los artículos... *(goods . . .)*
      de madera *(made of wood)*
      de oro *(made of gold)*
      de plata *(made of silver)*
      de lana *(made of wool)*
      de cuero *(made of leather)*
      de papel *(made of paper)*

    la artesanía *(crafts)*
    la cerámica *(ceramics)*

Práctica

Choose the most logical association for each item.

1. los aretes
    a. de papel   **b.** de oro   **c.** de lana

2. el anillo
    a. de oro   **b.** de cerámica   **c.** de madera

3. el suéter
    a. de lana   **b.** de papel   **c.** de madera

4. las joyas
    a. de plata   **b.** de lana   **c.** de papel

5. la escultura
    a. de lana   **b.** de cuero   **c.** de madera

Did You Get It? Answer Key

PRÁCTICA DE VOCABULARIO

LEGENDS AND STORIES, pp. 2–3

1
1. enemigo
2. mensaje
3. batallas
4. volcán
5. guerra
6. azteca

2
1. ejército
2. princesa
3. llorar
4. enemigo
5. enamorado
6. valiente

3
1. T	3. F	5. T
2. T	4. F	6. T

4 Una **[1. leyenda]** azteca

Una **[2. princesa]** vive en un gran palacio con su padre, el **[3. emperador]** azteca. La princesa es **[4. hermosa]**. Ella está **[5. enamorada]** de un **[6. guerrero]**. El querido es **[7. valiente]**. Es el más valiente del **[8. ejército]**. Pero un **[9. enemigo]** tiene **[10. celos]** de los dos porque él también está enamorado de la princesa. El guerrero valiente lucha en una **[11. batalla]** contra el enemigo. El enemigo muere. La princesa y el guerrero valiente **[12. se casan]**.

5
1. cansada	5. transformado
2. casado	6. ganadas
3. cerrada	7. enojados
4. entrenados	8. perdido

PRÁCTICA DE GRAMÁTICA

THE IMPERFECT TENSE, pp. 5–6

1. estaba
2. cantaban
3. escribía
4. hacíamos
5. salía
6. tenías
7. estudiaban
8. jugaban
9. comíais
10. vivíamos

Did You Get It? Answer Key

❷

1.

  a. veía

  b. veía

  c. veíais

  d. veíamos

  e. veían

2.

  a. ibas

  b. iba

  c. iban

  d. iba

  e. iban

3.

  a. eran

  b. era

  c. eran

  d. eras

  e. erais

❸

  1. jugaba

  2. hacíamos

  3. veíamos

  4. lloraban

  5. era

  6. íbamos

  7. veían

  8. salías

  9. practicaba

  10. enseñaba

❹

  1. era

  2. tenía

  3. vivía

  4. iba

  5. venía

  6. caminábamos (íbamos)

  7. trabajaban

  8. hacíamos

  9. jugábamos

  10. veíamos

  11. cenábamos

  12. dormíamos

❺ *Answers will vary.*

PRÁCTICA DE GRAMÁTICA

PRETERITE VS. IMPERFECT, pp. 8–9

❶

  1. P

  2. P

  3. I

  4. P

  5. I

  6. P

  7. P

  8. I

❷

  1. a

  2. b

  3. a

  4. b

  5. b

  6. b

Did You Get It? Answer Key

3

1. fuimos
2. estaba
3. era
4. fue
5. Llegamos
6. llevaba
7. jugamos
8. empezó
9. llegó
10. regaló
11. fue
12. pasamos

4

1. era
2. gustaba
3. prefería
4. llegó
5. estaba
6. quería
7. vimos

5

1. Ayer comí papas fritas.
2. El año pasado fui a México.
3. Cuando era joven, montaba en bicicleta.
4. Ellos estudiaban cuando la pizza llegó.
5. Cuando vivíamos en Boston, íbamos al parque todos los días.

 ¿RECUERDAS?

EXPRESSIONS OF FREQUENCY, p. 10

Práctica

Answers will vary.

¿RECUERDAS?

WEATHER EXPRESSIONS, p. 11

Práctica

1 *Answers will vary, but should include one logical weather expression for each season:*
La primavera: Hace frío. Llueve. Hace viento.
El verano: Hace calor. Hace sol.
El otoño: Hace viento. Hace sol.
El invierno: Hace frío. Nieva. Hace viento.

2 *Answers will vary.*

¿RECUERDAS?

DAILY ACTIVITIES, p. 12

Answers will vary.

Did You Get It? Answer Key

PRÁCTICA DE VOCABULARIO
EARLY AND MODERN CIVILIZATIONS, pp. 14–15

1

1. g
2. f
3. d
4. c
5. a
6. b
7. e

2

1. rascacielos
2. acera
3. semáforo
4. barrio
5. edificio

3

1. A
2. M
3. A
4. M
5. A
6. M
7. A

4

1. semáforos
2. calendario
3. avenida
4. templos
5. monumentos
6. cazaban
7. catedral
8. agricultura
9. edificio
10. barrio

5 *Answers will vary.*

Did You Get It? Answer Key

PRÁCTICA DE GRAMÁTICA

PRETERITE OF **-CAR**, **-GAR**, AND **-ZAR** VERBS, pp. 17–18

****

1.

1. crucé
2. cruzó
3. cruzamos
4. cruzaste
5. cruzaron

2.

1. pagaste
2. pagamos
3. pagó
4. pagaron
5. pagué

3.

1. sacamos
2. saqué
3. sacaron
4. sacasteis
5. sacó

❷

1. Si, comencé...
2. Sí, saqué ....
3. Sí, pagué....
4. Sí, almorcé...
5. Sí, toqué...
6. Sí, busqué...

❸

1. busqué
2. empecé
3. llegué
4. leyó
5. almorcé
6. construyeron
7. practiqué
8. toqué
9. organicé
10. apagué

❹ *Answers will vary.*

PRÁCTICA DE GRAMÁTICA

MORE VERBS WITH IRREGULAR PRETERITE STEMS, pp. 20–21

❶

1. c
2. b
3. a
4. a
5. b
6. c

❷

1. José trajo fotos de unas ruinas toltecas.
2. Marta y Andrea trajeron un collar azteca.
3. Yo traje un calendario mexicano muy antiguo.
4. Mi hermana y yo trajimos objetos de unas excavaciones en México.
5. Tú trajiste una escultura mexicana muy linda.

Did You Get It? Answer Key

❸

1. tomamos
2. quiso
3. dijo
4. traje
5. trajeron
6. vinimos

❹ *Answers will vary.*

✾ ¿RECUERDAS?
DAILY ACTIVITIES, p. 22

Práctica

Answers will vary.

✾ ¿RECUERDAS?
ARTS AND CRAFTS, p. 23

Práctica

1. b
2. a
3. a
4. a
5. c

Una leyenda *Práctica de vocabulario*

Identify the following two-word combinations from **Vocabulario** using the parts of the combinations shown in each box.

Vocabulario		
estar	emperador	enamorado(a)
enemigo	histórico(a)	montaña
heróico(a)	hermoso(a)	bello(a)
héroe	guerrero	valiente
siglos	narración	muchos

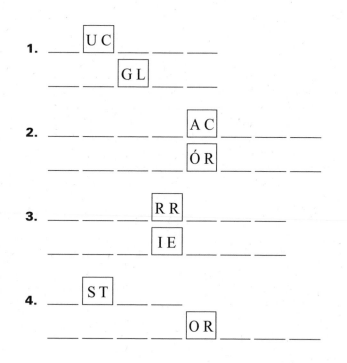

1. ___ U C ___ ___ ___

___ G L ___ ___

2. ___ ___ ___ ___ A C ___ ___

___ ___ ___ Ó R ___ ___

3. ___ ___ R R ___ ___ ___

___ ___ I E ___

4. ___ S T ___ ___

___ ___ ___ ___ O R ___

Dos puertas *Vocabulario en contexto*

Behind one door is the hero waiting to marry the princess. Behind another is the enemy waiting to kidnap the princess. Answer the questions below and unscramble the clue letters to help the princess choose the right door.

1. ¿Quién tiene celos de la princesa y el héroe?

____ ____   ____ ____ ____ ____ ____ ____ ____
         3   2

2. La princesa y el héroe se casan porque están

____ ____ ____ ____ ____ ____ ____ ____ ____ ____ .
                 5   4

3. ¿Dónde vive el emperador y la princesa?

____ ____   ____ ____ ____ ____ ____ ____
         1   6

Bonus: Which door should the princess choose? ____ ____ ____ ____ ____ ____
                                     1   2   3   4   5   6

Crucigrama *Práctica de gramática 1*

Complete the crossword puzzle with the logical verb in the imperfect tense.

Horizontal (*Across*)

3. Nosotros siempre _____ a casa a las tres de la tarde.

5. Yo _____ una película todos los días la semana pasada.

6. Nosotros _____ a pie a la escuela a las ocho el año pasado.

Abajo (*Down*)

1. De niño tú _____ celos de tu hermano.

2. Los jóvenes _____ enamorados.

4. El palacio del emperador _____ muy grande.

UNIDAD 4 Lección 1

Practice Games

Palabras confundidas *Gramática en contexto*

Unscramble the past participle words to complete the sentences.

1. Los jóvenes están TODVISNIA _____ .

2. La puerta está ADCARER _____ .

3. La princesa está RODDIAM _____ .

4. El guerrero está OTISDEV _____ .

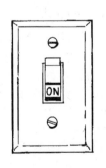

5. La luz está PADAGAA _____ .

6. La ropa está ALDAAV _____ .

7. El pastel está REDODCAO _____ .

Código secreto *Práctica de gramática 2*

Marisa used a secret code to write a story. Use the code key to decipher the legend and conjugate the verbs in the preterite or the imperfect.

★ : yo   ♥ : princesa   ☛ : los jóvenes

❖ : tú   ♣ : nosotros

Había una vez una ♥ _____ que (*tener*) _____

quince años. Un día la ♥ _____ (*salir*) _____ con

sus amigos. Todos ☛ _____ (*querer*) _____ subir

la montaña. "★ _____ (*subir*) _____ la montaña

el año pasado. Es peligroso," dijo (*said*) una chica. La ♥ _____ (*tener*)

_____ miedo. "❖ _____ (*ser*) _____

muy valiente. Quiero oír tu historia." Después, la ♥ _____

(*escuchar*) _____ la historia de la chica. ☛ _____ no

(*ir*) _____ a la montaña y ellos (*seguir*) _____ felices.

El alfabeto: A a Z *Todo junto*

Use the letters of the alphabet to complete these nine words from **Vocabulario**.
Use each letter only once.

A B C D E F G H I J L M N Ñ O P Q R S T U V Y Z

1. ____ e r s o n a ____ e

2. ____ é r o ____

3. ____ ____ e r ____ d a

4. m o ____ t a ____ a

5. ____ a ____ i e n t e

6. ____ i ____ l o

7. t ____ a n s ____ ____ r ____ a r

8. l e ____ e n ____ a

9. a ____ t e ____ ____

10. ____ a ____ a l l a

¿Qué haces? *Lectura*

Use the clues to fill in the missing letters of the imperfect or preterite verb conjugations to find out what these people are doing right now, what they usually do, or what they did.

1. Jaime y yo   h ___ b l ___ b ___ ___ ___ ___   por teléfono todos los días.

2. Lucia siempre   l ___ e ___ ___ b ___   a clase tarde.

3. Yo no   t ___ m ___   apuntes en la clase de ciencia ayer.

4. Teodoro y Andrés   c ___ n f ___ r m ___ ___ ___ ___   el vuelo anoche.

5. A veces tú   t ___ n ___ ___ ___   celos de tu hermana en las competiciones.

6. Ustedes siempre   r ___ g ___ t ___ ___ b ___ ___   bueno precios en el mercado.

7. Efraín   t ___ c ___ ___ ___   la guitarra todos los días.

Tienes... *Repaso de la lección*

Find the eight letters of the mystery word by solving the sentence puzzles.
Hint: circle all the letters that the two words from **Vocabulario** have in common
and cross out those that also appear in the third word.

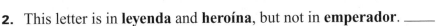

1. This letter is in **azteca** and **valiente**, but not in **batalla**. _____

2. This letter is in **leyenda** and **heroína**, but not in **emperador**. _____

3. This letter is in **hermosa** and **querida**, but not in **llorar**. _____

4. This letter is in **montaña** and **mensaje**, but not in **volcán**. _____

5. This letter is in **narración** and **siglo**, but not in **celos**. _____

6. This letter is in **guerra** and **enemigo**, but not in **jóven**. _____

7. This letter is in **sobre** and **dios**, but not in **mensaje**. _____

8. This letter is in **princesa** and **regresar**, but not in **pelear**. _____

Palabras escondidas *Práctica de vocabulario*

Use the following sentence to create words from the **Vocabulario**. There are at least
eleven possible answers. Can you find more? Hint: don't worry about accent marks.

Vieron las cuatro pirámides antiguas.

1. _____
2. _____
3. _____
4. _____
5. _____

6. _____
7. _____
8. _____
9. _____
10. _____

11. _____
12. _____
13. _____
14. _____
15. _____

UNIDAD 4 Lección 2

Practice Games

¡Al rescate! *Vocabulario en contexto*

The princess has been trapped in a labyrinth. Follow the directions into the labyrinth to find her and write the letter that corresponds to her location on the line below.

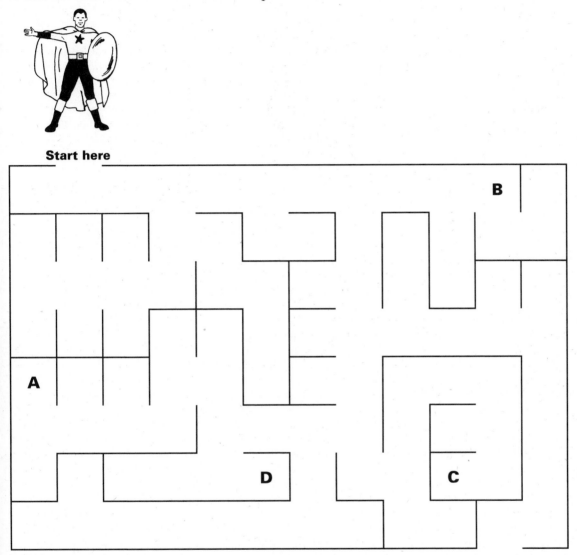

Start here

A   B   C   D

Debes doblar a la izquierda y seguir derecho. Al tercer pasillo (hallway), debes doblar a la derecha y seguir derecho. Debes doblar a la izquierda al fin del pasillo. Debes seguir derecho y luego debes doblar a la izquierda otra vez. Debes seguir derecho y al fin del pasillo, debes doblar a la derecha. Debes seguir derecho y doblar a la derecha al fin del pasillo. Debes seguir derecho a la princesa.

Where was the princess? _____

¿Que encontró el arqueólogo? *Práctica de gramática 1*

Write the preterite **yo** form of each verb on the lines. Then, circle the word that says what the archaeologist found.

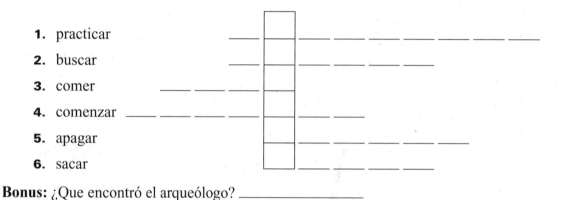

1. practicar   ___ | ___ ___ ___ ___ ___ ___ ___

2. buscar   ___ | ___ ___ ___ ___

3. comer   ___ ___ | ___ ___ ___

4. comenzar   ___ ___ ___ | ___ ___ ___

5. apagar | ___ ___ ___ ___ ___

6. sacar | ___ ___ ___ ___

Bonus: ¿Que encontró el arqueólogo? _____

UNIDAD 4 Lección 2

Practice Games

¿Qué hiciste? *Gramática en contexto*

Use the clues to fill in the missing letters of the preterite verb conjugations with spelling changes.

1. Yo p ____ g ____ ____ la cuenta y la propina con tarjeta de crédito.
2. Yo c ____ u ____ ____ la calle cuando el semáforo estaba en verde.
3. Yo p ____ s ____ ____ ____ un gran pescado para la cena.
4. Yo a l ____ ____ r ____ ____ en la cafetería con los amigos.
5. Yo p r ____ c ____ i ____ ____ ____ con el equipo ayer.

6. Yo n ____ v ____ g ____ ____ por Internet esta mañana.

7. Yo b ____ s ____ ____ ____ mis llaves y por fin las encontré.
8. Yo a p ____ g ____ ____ la luz del comedor después de comer.

Crucigrama *Práctica de gramática 2*

Use the correct preterite forms of **venir, traer, decir,** or **querer** to complete the sentences about Susana's party. Fill in the crossword puzzle.

Horizontal (*Across*)

1. Amalia _____ tarde a la fiesta.

2. Gabi y Fernando _____ ir a la fiesta pero no pudieron.

5. Tú _____ conmigo a la fiesta.

6. Tú _____ un pastel muy rico, también.

Abajo (*Down*)

1. Después todos nosotros _____ al salón para bailar.

2. Vosotros _____ bailar, pero la música era muy mala.

3. Yo _____ unos discos compactos nuevos de mi coche.

4. Yo le _____ a Mateo, «Cambia la música.»

Tic-Tac-Toe *Todo junto*

Alone or taking turns with a friend, find the forms of the preterite **venir**, **traer**, **decir**, or **querer** in the boxes to see which letter wins at Tic-Tac-Toe. Place an **O** on the board over the correct answer for number 1. Then allow a partner to place an **X** over number 2. Play until someone has won.

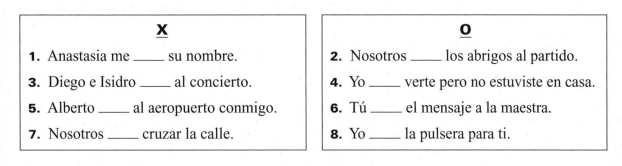

X	**O**
1. Anastasia me _____ su nombre.	**2.** Nosotros _____ los abrigos al partido.
3. Diego e Isidro _____ al concierto.	**4.** Yo _____ verte pero no estuviste en casa.
5. Alberto _____ al aeropuerto conmigo.	**6.** Tú _____ el mensaje a la maestra.
7. Nosotros _____ cruzar la calle.	**8.** Yo _____ la pulsera para ti.

trajimos	traje	vinieron
viniste	dijiste	quise
vino	quisimos	dijo

Who won? _____

Mi libro es... *Lectura cultural*

Figure out the seven-letter word that describes your Spanish textbook. Hint: circle all the letters that the two words from **Vocabulario** have in common and then eliminate those that are also in the third word.

Mi libro es ____ ____ ____ ____ ____ ____ ____ .

1. This letter is in **tumba** and **semáforo**, but not in **ciudad**. ____

2. This letter is in **barrio** and **antiguo**, but not in **esquina**. ____
3. This letter is in **avenida** and **catedral**, but not in **acera**. ____

4. This letter is in **moderno** and **frente**, but not in **ruina**. ____
5. This letter is in **religión** and **pirámide**, but not in **excavación**. ____
6. This letter is in **herramienta** and **antigua**, but not in **agricultura**. ____
7. This letter is in **monumento** and **objeto**, but not in **estatua**. ____

UNIDAD 4 Lección 2

Practice Games

44

Unidad 4, Lección 2
Practice Games

¡Avancemos! 2
Unit Resource Book

Ciudad loca *Repaso de la lección*

There is something wrong with this city. Look at the picture and list all of the things you find that are wrong or don't make sense.

1. _____

2. _____

3. _____

4. _____

5. _____

6. _____

7. _____

Practice Games Answer Key

PAGE 30

Practica de vocabulario

1. muchos siglos
2. narración histórica
3. guerrero valiente
4. estar enamorado(a)

PAGE 31

Vocabulario en contexto

1. el enemigo
2. enamorados
3. el (un) palacio

Bonus: PIEDRA

PAGE 32

Práctica de gramática 1

1. tenías
2. estaban
3. regresábamos
4. era
5. veía
6. íbamos

PAGE 33

Gramática en contexto

1. invitados
2. cerrada
3. dormida
4. vestido
5. apagada
6. lavada
7. decorado

Practice Games Answer Key

Práctica de gramática 2

1. princesa / tenía
2. princesa / salió
3. los jóvenes / querían
4. Yo / subí
5. princesa / tenía
6. Tú / fuiste
7. princesa / escuchó
8. Los jóvenes / fueron / siguieron

Todo junto

1. personaje
2. héroe
3. querida
4. montaña
5. valiente
6. siglo
7. transformar
8. leyenda
9. azteca
10. batalla

Lectura

1. hablábamos
2. llegaba
3. tomé
4. confirmaron
5. tenías
6. regateaban
7. tocaba

Repaso de la lección

1. E
2. N
3. E
4. M
5. I
6. G
7. O
8. S

UNIDAD 4 Lección 1   Practice Games Answer Key

Practice Games Answer Key

PAGE 38
Práctica de vocabulario

1. catedral
2. acera
3. cuadra
4. avenida
5. antiguo / antigua
6. moderno / moderna
7. ruina
8. templo
9. religión
10. agriculturo / agricultora
11. calendario
12. estatua
13. construir
14. toltecas
15. agricultura
16. entre

PAGE 39
Vocabulario en contexto

1. C

PAGE 40
Práctica de gramática 1

1. practiqué
2. busqué
3. comí
4. comencé
5. apagué
6. saqué

BONUS: ruinas

PAGE 41
Gramática en contexto

1. pagué
2. crucé
3. pesqué
4. almorcé
5. practiqué
6. navegué
7. busqué
8. apagué

UNIDAD 4 Lección 2

Practice Games Answer Key

Unidad 4, Lección 2
Practice Games Answer Key

48

¡Avancemos! 2
Unit Resource Book

Practice Games Answer Key

PAGE 42

Práctica de gramática 2

Horizontal

1. vino
2. quisieron
5. viniste
6. trajiste

Vertical

1. vinimos
2. quisisteis
3. traje
4. dije

PAGE 43

Todo junto

1. dijo
2. trajimos
3. vinieron
4. quise
5. vino
6. dijiste
7. quisimos
8. (traje)

Bonus: X

PAGE 44

Lectura cultural

1. M
2. O
3. D
4. E
5. R
6. N
7. O

PAGE 45

Repaso de la lección

1. Hay una pirámide en la cuidad moderna.
2. El edificio tiene un semáforo por una ventana.
3. La joyería tiene un letrero para la librería.
4. Hay un edificio en la calle.
5. Hay un volcán en el rascacielo.
6. El perro lleva ropa.
7. La policía lleva un zapato y una sandalia.

Video Activities *Vocabulario*

PRE-VIEWING ACTIVITY

Create a legend and write a short paragraph describing the conflict. Who is the hero? The heroine? The enemy? What is the conflict? How does the conflict get resolved?

_____

_____

_____

_____

_____

_____

VIEWING ACTIVITY

Read the following elements of a legend. While you watch the video write **sí** next to each element that appears in the story.

_____ **1.** un emperador

_____ **2.** un guerrero

_____ **3.** un ejército

_____ **4.** una heroína

_____ **5.** un dios

_____ **6.** un enemigo

_____ **7.** una batalla

_____ **8.** un volcán

_____ **9.** una montaña

_____ **10.** un palacio

UNIDAD 4 Lección 1

Video Activities

50

Unidad 4, Lección 1
Video Activities

¡Avancemos! 2
Unit Resource Book

Video Activities *Vocabulario*

POST-VIEWING ACTIVITY

Complete each sentence with the best word from the box.

casados	enamorados	celos	una guerra	mensaje	palacio	sueño
	volcán	bello	hermosa		triste	valiente

1. El héroe es muy _____.

2. La heroína es una princesa y es muy _____.

3. El héroe y la heroína están _____.

4. El enemigo tiene _____.

5. El héroe y el enemigo pelean en _____.

6. Al final todos los personajes regresan al _____.

Video Activities *Telehistoria escena 1*

PRE-VIEWING ACTIVITY

Answer the following questions about writing assignments.

1 What are four steps that a person should take before writing a research paper or a creative writing project?

1. _____

2. _____

3. _____

4. _____

2 Did you use the four steps listed in number one on your last writing assignment? If so, did this help you write a good paper?

_____

_____

3 Do you think brainstorming for ideas is more productive in a group of people or alone?

_____

_____

4 Why or why not?

_____

_____

VIEWING ACTIVITY

Read the sentences below before watching the video. Then, while you watch the video, indicate with a checkmark (✓) if you hear spoken or implied each of the following sentences.

_____ ¿Por qué no hacemos una leyenda sobre un ejército?

_____ Tiene que ser cómica.

_____ ¿Conoces una leyenda mexicana?

_____ Hay una leyenda sobre aquella ciudad histórica.

_____ Yo conozco esa leyenda.

_____ Queremos oírla.

Video Activities *Telehistoria escena 1*

POST-VIEWING ACTIVITY

Indicate whether each of the following statements is true (T) or false (F).

1. Los chicos son de México.   T   F

2. Todos quieren hacer una película sobre una leyenda romántica.   T   F

3. El guía conoce la leyenda sobre los volcanes en el parque.   T   F

4. El guía empieza contarles la leyenda a los chicos.   T   F

5. Hay tres personajes en la leyenda: un emperador, la hija del   T   F
   emperador y un tolteca.

6. La princesa se llamaba María.   T   F

Video Activities *Telehistoria escena 2*

PRE-VIEWING ACTIVITY

What is your favorite fairy tale or legend? Write an important passage from this story below. When you finish, pass your worksheet to the person on your left. Can he or she guess the title of the story?

_____

_____

_____

_____

_____

_____

_____

_____

_____

_____

_____

_____

_____

VIEWING ACTIVITY

Read the following statements before watching the video. Then, while watching the video, choose the person or people to fill in the blank and write the appropriate letter. One answer is used more than once.

a. **el emperador**

b. **Popocatépetl**

c. **Ixtaccíhuatl**

d. **Ixtaccíhuatl** y **Popocatépetl**.

_____ Muchos estaban enamorados de _____.

_____ _____ era un guerrero valiente.

_____ _____ ya era muy viejo.

_____ Los volcanes llevan los nombres de _____.

_____ _____ se fue a pelear pero regresó rápidamente.

UNIDAD 4 Lección 1

Video Activities

Video Activities *Telehistoria escena 2*

POST-VIEWING ACTIVITY

Choose the word or phrase that best completes each of the following sentences, according to the **Telehistoria**.

ejército	diosa	valiente	heroína	tener celos	batallas
enemigos	morir	casarse	aztecas	regresar	hermosa

1. La princesa era muy _____.

2. Ixta es la _____ de la leyenda.

3. Popo llevó a su _____ a una guerra.

4. La guerra era contra sus _____.

5. El emperador peleó en muchas _____.

6. Ixta quería _____ con Popo.

7. Para casarse con Ixta, Popo debía ser _____.

8. Popo tenía que _____ porque Ixta era muy triste sin él.

Video Activities *Telehistoria escena 3*

PRE-VIEWING ACTIVITY

At the end of the last **Telehistoria** episode, Popocatépetl and Ixtaccíhuatl wanted to get married. How do you think this legend will end? Write two possible endings to this story in the spaces provided below.

A sad ending to the story:

A happy ending to the story:

VIEWING ACTIVITY

Read the list of events below before watching the video. Then, while you watch the video, put the events in the correct order.

_____ La princesa murió.

_____ Popo llevó Ixta a una montaña muy alta.

_____ Popo ganó la guerra.

_____ El otro guerrero les dijo a todos que Popo murió.

_____ Los dioses transformaron a Popo e Ixta en dos volcanes.

_____ Popo volvió.

_____ Otro guerrero regresó al palacio antes de Popo.

Video Activities *Telehistoria escena 3*

POST-VIEWING ACTIVITY

Circle the word that best completes each sentence.

1. Otro guerrero llevaba / tenía celos de Popo.

2. El otro guerrero regresó al palacio primero / segundo y dijo que Popo murió.

3. El otro guerrero estaba enojado / enamorado de Ixta.

4. La princesa estaba tan heroica / triste que murió.

5. Popo volvió al palacio y transformó / encontró a Ixta.

6. Popo llevó a la princesa a la montaña / pantalla más alta.

7. De vez en cuando se despierta el volcán que se llama Popo y llora / canta por la princesa.

Video Activities *Vocabulario*

PRE-VIEWING ACTIVITY

Place a (✓) next to the following sites that you have seen in your community or during a trip. Write the name and briefly describe the place where you saw each site.

——— un rascacielos _____

——— una catedral _____

——— una tumba _____

——— una plaza _____

——— unas ruinas _____

——— un templo _____

——— una pirámide _____

——— un monumento _____

——— una estatua _____

——— unas excavaciones _____

VIEWING ACTIVITY

Read the list of attractions before watching the video. Then watch the video. Place **(1)** beside the attractions that you can see in or near the **Zócalo**, and **(2)** beside the attractions that you can see in the **Museo Nacional de Antropología**.

1. El Zócalo **2. El Museo Nacional de Antropología**

——— catedral ——— monumento

——— rascacielos ——— cerámica

——— tesoro antiguo ——— herramienta

——— escultura ——— estatua

Video Activities *Vocabulario*

POST-VIEWING ACTIVITY

Choose the word or phrase that best completes each of the following sentences.

1. La Ciudad de México es una ciudad _____.
   - **a.** moderna
   - **b.** pequeña
   - **c.** saludable

2. El Templo Mayor es el gran templo de _____.
   - **a.** los toltecas
   - **b.** los agricultores
   - **c.** los aztecas

3. En el Templo Mayor había grandes _____.
   - **a.** pirámides
   - **b.** rascacielos
   - **c.** semáforos

4. El Museo Nacional de Antropología está en _____.
   - **a.** el Templo Mayor
   - **b.** el Zócalo
   - **c.** el parque Chapultepec

5. Jorge dice que desayunó hace siglos porque _____.
   - **a.** su comida era como la de los aztecas
   - **b.** comió hace mucho tiempo
   - **c.** sus padres son aztecas

Video Activities *Telehistoria escena 1*

PRE-VIEWING ACTIVITY

Imagine that you are home from school sick and your cousin is running errands for you. Give your cousin directions from your house to the following places:

school:

the library:

the video store:

VIEWING ACTIVITY

Below are the directions Beto, Jorge, and Sandra need to follow in order to get to the movie theater. Read all the directions before you watch the video. Then put the directions in the correct order while you watch. *Caution: There are only four directions they need to follow to get to the movie theater.*

_____ seguir derecho hasta el rascacielos

_____ caminar dos cuadras

_____ ir hasta el siguiente semáforo

_____ doblar a la izquierda

_____ cruzar la calle Diana

_____ doblar a la derecha

Video Activities *Telehistoria escena 1*

POST-VIEWING ACTIVITY

How would Beto, Jorge, Sandra, or the woman in the street answer each of the following questions? Choose the most appropriate answer to each question.

1. ¿Está el cine Diana en este barrio? _____

2. ¿Dónde queda el cine? _____

3. ¿Por qué van al cine? Está cerrado. _____

4. ¿Es para el colegio esta excursión? _____

5. ¿A qué hora llega el autobús? _____

6. ¿Por qué van ustedes a la derecha? _____

a. No. Vamos solamente porque queremos saber más sobre la historia de México.

b. Sí, es verdad. Tenemos que doblar a la izquierda.

c. Ay, ¡muy pronto! Nos tenemos que ir.

d. Sí. Está muy cerca de ese rascacielos.

e. Vamos a la parada de autobuses frente al cine.

f. Está en una esquina. Tienen que doblar a la izquierda, caminar dos cuadras y luego doblar a la derecha.

Video Activities *Telehistoria escena 2*

PRE-VIEWING ACTIVITY

Answer the following questions about United States history.

1 Write down one fact that you know about the land and the people of the United States in pre-historic times.

2 Where could you find out more about our ancient history?

3 Write down one fact that you know about the history of the United States.

4 What is one thing you know about the history of your state?

5 Where could you find out more about the history of your state?

VIEWING ACTIVITY

Read the following list of activities before watching the video. Then, while watching the video, check off (✓) the activities that were done by the culture that Beto, Sandra, and Jorge visit.

_____ Hacían cerámica.

_____ Regateaban.

_____ Hacían agricultura.

_____ Tenían gran ejércitos.

_____ Se casaban con dioses.

_____ Construyeron pirámides.

_____ Hacían herramientas.

_____ Hacían esculturas de dioses.

_____ Cazaban.

_____ Construyeron monumentos.

Video Activities *Telehistoria escena 2*

POST-VIEWING ACTIVITY

Indicate whether each of the following statements is true (T) or false (F).

1. La civilización de los aztecas es más antigua que la civilización de los toltecas. T F

2. Hace muchos siglos construyeron pirámides los toltecas. T F

3. Los toltecas solamente cazaban animales pequeños. T F

4. Los toltecas eran grandes militares. T F

5. Los toltecas solo hacían cerámica el Día de los Dioses. T F

6. Jorge dice que la estatua está preocupada. T F

7. Sandra cree que la estatua no almorzó. T F

8. Jorge piensa que la estatua sacó una mala nota en la clase de ciencias. T F

9. Beto dice que la estatua pagó demasiado por su sombrero. T F

Video Activities *Telehistoria escena 3*

PRE-VIEWING ACTIVITY

You are the organizer of a treasure hunt. You have to write a key describing where you have placed each of the following objects. Write the directions from a neighborhood park to each of the following places.

❶ object: crystal vase
location: the fireplace mantel (or furnace) at your house

_____

_____

❷ object: miniature King Tut tomb
location: on the librarian's desk in the school library

_____

_____

_____

_____

❸ object: rose in the mouth of an equestrian statue
location: at your town or city hall

_____

_____

VIEWING ACTIVITY

Read the following statements before watching the video. Then, while watching the video, indicate with a checkmark (✓) if one of the characters says or is likely to say each statement.

_____ Tenemos que regresar al autobús.

_____ Jorge estaba aquí cuando fui a comprar una bebida.

_____ Encontré una herramienta.

_____ Quería tomar un foto del templo cuando lo vi.

_____ Cuando crucé la plaza lo encontré.

_____ ¡Es de una civilización muy antigua!

_____ Está hecho a mano.

UNIDAD 4 Lección 2

Video Activities

Unidad 4, Lección 2
Video Activities

64

¡Avancemos! 2
Unit Resource Book

Video Activities *Telehistoria escena 3*

POST-VIEWING ACTIVITY

Choose the word(s) that best complete(s) each of the following sentences.

1. Los jóvenes deben estar en casa _____.

   a. a las siete

   b. a las seis

   c. a las cinco

2. Después de pocos minutos _____ Jorge.

   a. pasea

   b. regresa

   c. pelea

3. Sandra fue a comprar _____.

   a. un recuerdo

   b. un objeto

   c. un refresco

4. Beto pregunta si el objeto es _____.

   a. un tesoro

   b. un plato

   c. un monumento

5. La guía dijo que el objeto era de una civilización _____.

   a. avanzada

   b. antigua

   c. moderna

6. La artesanía fue hecha en México _____.

   a. hace muchos siglos

   b. en el siglo pasado

   c. en 2006

Video Activities Answer Key

VOCABULARIO pp. 50–51

PRE-VIEWING ACTIVITY

Answers will vary. Possible answer: Andrew is the hero of my story. He loves the princess Lena, but her father is a wicked emperor and won't allow them to marry. Andrew and Lena run away but are tracked down by Lena's father. Lena calls for help and her mother, the goddess of nature, turns Lena's father into a large rock.

VIEWING ACTIVITY

1. sí		**2.** sí	
4. sí		**6.** sí	
7. sí		**10.** sí	

POST-VIEWING ACTIVITY

1. valiente	**4.** celos
2. hermosa	**5.** una guerra
3. enamorados	**6.** palacio

TELEHISTORIA ESCENA 1 pp. 52–53

PRE-VIEWING ACTIVITY

1. *Answers will vary. Possible answers:* 1. brainstorm 2. find the main idea or thesis of the topic 3. research 4. create an outline

2. *Answers will vary. Possible answer:* I did use all of these steps, and I received a good grade on my last paper.

3. *Answers will vary. Possible answer:* I think brainstorming with a group of people is more productive than working alone.

4. *Answers will vary. Possible answer:* I think it is more productive to brainstorm in a group because you get the ideas of more people—this helps you come up with more ideas in a shorter period of time.

VIEWING ACTIVITY

¿Por qué no hacemos una leyenda sobre un ejército?

Tiene que ser cómica.

¿Conoces una leyenda mexicana? ✓

Hay una leyenda sobre aquella ciudad histórica.

Yo conozco esa leyenda. ✓

Queremos oírla. ✓

POST-VIEWING ACTIVITY

1. T		**3.** T		**5.** F	
2. F		**4.** T		**6.** F	

TELEHISTORIA ESCENA 2 pp. 54–55

PRE-VIEWING ACTIVITY

Answers will vary. Possible answer: Once upon a time there was a young, beautiful girl who lived with her evil stepmother and stepsisters. She worked very hard all day and all night long. She found out that there was a ball at the town castle and she asked her stepmother if she could go. Her stepmother told her that she could go only if she had a dress to wear.

VIEWING ACTIVITY

Muchos estaban enamorados de **[c]**.

[b] era un guerrero valiente.

[a] ya era muy viejo.

Los volcanes están llamados por **[d]**.

[b] se fue a pelear pero regresó rápidamente.

POST-VIEWING ACTIVITY

1. hermosa		**5.** batallas	
2. heroína		**6.** casarse	
3. ejército		**7.** valiente	
4. enemigos		**8.** regresar	

TELEHISTORIA ESCENA 3 pp. 56–57

PRE-VIEWING ACTIVITY

A sad ending to the story: *Answers will vary. Possible answer:* After getting married, Popo goes back to war. He fights bravely, but in the last day of battle he is fatally injured. The news of his death reaches Ixta soon after. She is so heartbroken that she decides to climb a volcano and jump to her death. Popo and Ixta are now buried at the site of the two volcanoes.

A happy ending to the story: *Answers will vary. Possible answer:* Popo goes back to battle. He and the army fight so well that the battle is over in one day. They march home and find that the entire village has already heard about their victory. There are parades and festivities for three full days. The village proclaims Popo the hero of their land and two volcanoes are named after him and Ixta. The two marry and live happily ever after.

VIEWING ACTIVITY

La princesa murió. **4**

Popo llevó Ixta a una montaña muy alta. **6**

Popo ganó la guerra. **1**

El otro guerrero les dijo a todos que Popo murió. **3**

Los dioses transformaron a Popo y Ixta en dos volcanes. **7**

Popo volvió. **5**

Otro guerrero regresó al palacio antes de Popo. **2**

POST-VIEWING ACTIVITY

1. tenía

2. primero

3. enamorado

4. triste

5. encontró

6. montaña

7. llora

Video Activities Answer Key

VOCABULARIO pp. 58–59

PRE-VIEWING ACTIVITY

Answers will vary.

VIEWING ACTIVITY

1. catedral, rascacielos, monumento, estatua
2. tesoro antiguo, escultura, cerámica, herramienta

POST-VIEWING ACTIVITY

1. a   4. c
2. c   5. b
3. a

TELEHISTORIA ESCENA 1 pp. 60–61

PRE-VIEWING ACTIVITY

school: *Answers will vary. Possible answer:* Turn left out of the driveway and go straight for seven blocks until you get to Lamar street. Turn left on Lamar Street and go past the post office. Turn left two street lights after the post office. My school is five blocks on the right.

the library: *Answers will vary. Possible answer:* Turn right out of my driveway and head toward Interstate 5. Go past the highway and turn left on Justin Lane. The library is two blocks up, across from the soccer fields.

the video store: *Answers will vary. Possible answer:* Turn left onto Davis Road. Go straight for ten blocks. The movie store is on the right-hand side of the road, across from Big Burgers.

VIEWING ACTIVITY

seguir derecho hasta el rascacielos

caminar dos cuadras **2**

ir hasta el siguiente semáforo **4**

doblar a la izquierda **1**

cruzar la calle Diana

doblar a la derecha **3**

POST-VIEWING ACTIVITY

1. d
2. f
3. e
4. a
5. c
6. b

TELEHISTORIA ESCENA 2 pp. 62–63

PRE-VIEWING ACTIVITY

1. *Answers will vary. Possible answer:* I know that there were a lot of American Indians who lived in our country.
2. *Answers will vary. Possible answer:* I could find out more about our ancient history in the library or at a natural science museum.
3. *Answers will vary. Possible answer:* George Washington was the first president of the United States.
4. *Answers will vary. Possible answer:* I know that it was one of the thirteen original colonies.
5. *Answers will vary. Possible answer:* I could find out more about the history of my state at the State History Museum or by doing research on the Internet.

VIEWING ACTIVITY

Hacían cerámica. ✓

Regateaban

Hacían agricultura. ✓

Tenían gran ejércitos. ✓

Se casaban con dioses.

Construyeron pirámides. ✓

Hacían herramientas.

Hacían esculturas de dioses. ✓

Cazaban. ✓

Construyeron monumentos. ✓

POST-VIEWING ACTIVITY

1. F
2. T
3. F
4. T
5. F
6. F
7. T
8. F
9. T

TELEHISTORIA ESCENA 3 pp. 64–65

PRE-VIEWING ACTIVITY

1. *Answers will vary. Possible answer:* Turn left on Guadalupe Street and go straight until you cross Broadway. The next street is Valley Ridge Road. Turn left. My house is on the corner.

2. *Answers will vary. Possible answer:* Turn right on Guadalupe Street. Stay on this street until you see our school on the right corner of Victory Lane. Walk through the school entrance and turn left on the sidewalk in front of the cafeteria. Follow the breezeway until you see a blue building. That is the library. The librarian's desk is the first thing you see as you enter the library.

3. *Answers will vary. Possible answer:* Turn right on Guadalupe Street. Turn left at Republic Square. The Town Hall is on the corner.

VIEWING ACTIVITY

Tenemos que regresar al autobús. ✓

Jorge estaba aquí cuando fui a comprar una bebida. ✓

Encontré una herramienta.

Quería tomar un foto del templo cuando lo vi. ✓

Cuando crucé la plaza lo encontré. ✓

¡Es de una civilización muy antigua!

Está hecho a mano.

POST-VIEWING ACTIVITY

1. b
2. b
3. c
4. a
5. a
6. c

Video Scripts

VOCABULARIO

Beto: Cuando lees o cuentas una leyenda...

Sandra: ...siempre empieza así:

Jorge: Había una vez...

Beto: En esta leyenda, los personajes son, un emperador, un guerrero —es muy valiente. ¡Es el héroe!

Jorge: ¿No necesito una heroína?

Beto: ¡Por supuesto! La heroína es una princesa muy hermosa. El héroe ve a la heroína. Él está enamorado de ella. Ella está enamorada de él. Pero allí viene el enemigo. Él tiene celos del héroe.

Jorge: Se lleva a la princesa. Entonces pelean. Hay una batalla; una guerra.

Sandra: Y la heroína gana.

Jorge: El héroe y la heroína se casan.

Beto: O el héroe muere. Y la heroína llora. Ella llora.

Sandra: El héroe no muere y la heroína no llora.

Beto: Sí, el héroe muere.

Sandra: Está bien. Entonces la heroína muere.

Jorge: ¿Qué? ¡El enemigo no puede ganar! Mejor, regresan al palacio a tomarse un refresco. Entonces, ¿cuál es el mensaje de esta leyenda?

Beto: No pelear con mujeres.

TELEHISTORIA
ESCENA 1

Sandra: ¿Una leyenda cómica?

Jorge: No. Una leyenda sobre México. Sobre nuestra historia. No tiene que ser cómica.

Beto: ¿Conoces una leyenda mexicana?

Sandra: Hay una leyenda sobre aquellos volcanes pero no la conozco.

Guía: Yo conozco esa leyenda. ¿Cómo están?

Sandra: ¿De veras? Queremos oírla.

Guía: Claro. Había una vez un emperador azteca. Su hija, la princesa, se llamaba Ixtaccíhuatl.

Jorge: Ixta...Ixtacc... Ay, ¡qué difícil! ¿Por qué no se llamaba María?

Video Scripts

TELEHISTORIA
ESCENA 2

Guía: La princesa Ixtaccíhuatl— bueno, mejor vamos a llamarla Ixta— era muy hermosa, y muchos hombres estaban enamorados de ella.

Sandra: Ixta, la heroína.

Guía: Popocatépetl, también conocido como Popo.

Sandra: Ah...sí...¡los nombres de los volcanes!

Guía: ¡Exactamente! Popo era un guerrero valiente del emperador y un día llevó a su ejército a una guerra contra el enemigo.

Beto: ¿Cómo? ¿El emperador no era valiente? ¿Por qué no quería pelear él?

Guía: Él peleó en muchas batallas, pero ya era muy viejo. El emperador le dijo: «Para casarte con mi hija, la princesa, debes ser valiente en la batalla y ganar la guerra.»

Jorge: ¿Si? ¿Casarse así? ¿Sin dinero u oro?

Guía: Popocatépetl estaba enamorado de Ixtaccíhuatl, y ella estaba enamorada de él. Cuando Popo se fue a la batalla, la princesa Ixta estaba triste y lloró. Popo tenía que regresar para casarse con ella.

Jorge: ¡Ay! ¡Mujeres!

TELEHISTORIA ESCENA 3

Guía: Popo fue muy valiente y ganó la guerra. Pero otro guerrero tenía celos de Popo y regresó al palacio primero diciendo que Popo murió en la guerra.

Jorge: ¿Por qué hizo eso?

Guía: Porque él también estaba enamorado de la princesa.

Jorge: ¡Que horror!

Guía: La princesa Ixta estaba tan triste que murió.

Jorge: ¡No puede ser!

Guía: Cuando Popo volvió al palacio encontró a la princesa. La llevó a la montaña más alta, donde los dioses transformaron al guerrero y a su princesa en dos volcanes, uno al lado del otro. Ixta está tranquila pero a menudo Popo se despierta y llora por ella. Esta es la leyenda de estos dos volcanes.

Sandra: ¡Qué leyenda buena!

Jorge: Sandra, tenías razón. Creo que debemos hacer una leyenda cómica.

Video Scripts

VOCABULARIO

Sandra: La Ciudad de México es una ciudad moderna pero con mucha historia. ¡Mira!

Beto: Este barrio es Polanco y es parte del D.F., el Distrito Federal.

Jorge: Y esto es el Zócalo, la plaza principal de la Ciudad de México.

Sandra: Aquí pueden ver las catedrales, los rascacielos.

Jorge: Las ruinas, las estatuas, y los monumentos.

Beto: En el Zócalo está el Templo Mayor. Pero, ¿cómo se llega allí?

Jorge: ¿Al Templo Mayor? Muy fácil. Debes ir a la esquina, allí donde está el semáforo. Cruzas la calle. Caminas una cuadra. Doblas a la izquierda.

Sandra: ¿A la izquierda? No, doblas a la derecha.

Jorge: Sí, sí, doblas a la derecha y caminas una cuadra más. Allí está.

Beto: Aquí está el Templo Mayor, el gran templo de los aztecas.

Sandra: Hace muchos siglos, los aztecas tenían ritos religiosos y hacían ceremonias para sus dioses aquí.

Jorge: Y había grandes pirámides.

Beto: No lejos de aquí está el parque de Chapultepec.

Sandra: Esto es el Museo Nacional de Antropología. Aquí pueden ver tesoros antiguos, esculturas, cerámicas, herramientas y mucho más.

Beto: Y ésa es la historia de México. ¿Qué hacemos ahora?

Jorge: Vamos a comer. Tengo hambre.

Beto: Pero, ¿no desayunaste?

Jorge: Sí, pero desayuno fue hace siglos. Ahora estamos en el presente y quiero almorzar ya.

TELEHISTORIA ESCENA 1

Beto: Perdón, ¿está el cine Diana en este barrio?

Mujer: Sí. Cerca de ese rascacielos.

Jorge: ¿Cómo llegamos allí? ¿Seguimos derecho?

Mujer: Deben doblar a la izquierda y caminar dos cuadras. Después doblan a la derecha y van al siguiente semáforo. El cine está en la esquina pero está cerrado.

Sandra: No vamos al cine, vamos a la parada de autobuses frente al cine. Vamos para Tula.

Mujer: ¡A Tula! ¿A ver las ruinas? ¿Es para el colegio?

Jorge: No, no. Hace unos días que filmamos una película sobre leyendas mexicanas, y ahora queremos saber más sobre la historia de México.

Mujer: ¡Fantástico! ¿A qué hora sale el autobús?

Sandra: Muy pronto. ¡Gracias! ¡A la izquierda!

Video Scripts

TELEHISTORIA ESCENA 2

Guía Turística: ¡Bienvenidos a Tula! Hace muchos siglos, antes de los aztecas, una civilización muy antigua, los toltecas, construyó estas pirámides y monumentos.

Beto: ¡Es una estatua de mi tío!

Sandra: ¡Sshh!

Guía Turística: No sabemos mucho sobre la gente de Tula. Sabemos que eran grandes militares, algunos cazaban y otros eran agricultores. Hacían cerámica y esculturas de dioses, como ésta.

Jorge: No está muy alegre, ¿verdad?

Sandra: No, creo que no almorzó.

Jorge: O que sacó una mala nota en la clase de matemáticas.

Beto: O que pagó demasiado por ese sombrero.

TELEHISTORIA COMPLETA

Beto: Tenemos que regresar. Debemos estar en casa a las seis.

Sandra: ¿Dónde está Jorge? Estaba aquí cuando fui a comprar un refresco.

Beto: Allí está.

Jorge: ¡Eh! Encontré algo: un objeto.

Beto: ¿Qué es? ¿Una herramienta antigua? ¿Un tesoro?

Sandra: ¿Dónde lo encontraste?

Jorge: Pues, yo estaba allí. Quería tomar una foto del templo pero no podía verlo bien desde aquí. Cuando crucé la plaza, encontré el objeto.

Official: Ya pude limpiarlo un poco. Es de una civilización muy avanzada.

Jorge: ¿De verdad?

Official: Sí, sí, dice: «Hecho en México, 2006.»

COMPARACIÓN CULTURAL VIDEO

Most Spanish-speaking cities were founded more than four hundred years ago. Some traditions and influences have become part of today's everyday life. Here we are going to show you an ancient religious tradition in Mexico that now is an artistic act, and several religious influences on the architecture of Toledo, Spain.

Mexico

These are the Papantla Flyers from Mexico. They perform a pre-Hispanic Totonacan fertility ritual dedicated to the Sun God. The flyers strap themselves from the waist and make 52 turns around the pole, one for every week of their solar calendar. After the arrival of the Spanish in Mexico, these rites were disguised as games. Today, this former religious act is considered a Mexican legacy.

Spain (Toledo)

The city of Toledo, Spain was founded by the Romans around 192 B.C. Today it is considered not only an important city from the medieval and Gothic periods, but a World Heritage Site by the United Nations.

The Moors lived in Spain for eight hundred years, and they had a major influence on Spanish culture and architecture. The **Puerta de la Bisagra** is one of the most impressive legacies of the region.

Toledo also shows Jewish architectural influences, like **Sinagoga del Tránsito** from the early 14th century.

One of the most spectacular buildings in Toledo is the Cathedral. The original Gothic structure was begun in 1226, but additions in different styles were made over the next five centuries.

Every country changes with time, but there are certain religious traditions and influences that live on. Here you saw a millenarian ritual to the Sun God in Mexico that now is an artistic act performed in plazas, and you also explored some ancient architecture in Spain worth visiting today. How far back can you trace the history of your city?

Audio Scripts

UNIDAD 4, LECCIÓN 1
TEXTBOOK SCRIPTS
TXT CD 5

PRESENTACIÓN DE VOCABULARIO

Level 2 Textbook pp. 198-199

TXT CD 5, Track 1

A. ¿Sabes lo que es una leyenda? Es una narración histórica que cuenta algo de la historia de un lugar o de unas personas. Para contar una leyenda, empiezas con la frase «Había una vez...». Vamos a conocer una leyenda azteca sobre dos jóvenes, los celos y la historia de dos volcanes.

B. Primero, presentamos a los personajes de nuestra leyenda. El héroe es un guerrero valiente. La heroína es la princesa. Es muy bella, o hermosa. El personaje malo es el enemigo.

C. El emperador vive con su hija querida, la princesa, en el palacio.

D. La princesa y el guerrero están enamorados. El enemigo tiene celos de los dos jóvenes porque él también está enamorado de la princesa.

E. En nuestra leyenda hay una guerra. El ejército del emperador pelea con los enemigos en una batalla.

F. ¿Cómo va a terminar la leyenda? ¿Regresa el héroe a su princesa querida? ¿Llora la princesa? ¿Se casan los dos? ¡Vamos a ver en la Telehistoria!

¡A RESPONDER!

Level 2 Textbook p. 199

TXT CD 5, Track 2

Escucha las siguientes oraciones. Imita la acción o al personaje que escuchas.

1. La heroína llora.
2. El guerrero pelea.
3. Yo llevo a la princesa.
4. Estoy enamorado.
5. Soy el héroe.
6. La montaña es alta.
7. Leo la leyenda.

TELEHISTORIA ESCENA 1

Level 2 Textbook p. 201

TXT CD 5, Track 3

Sandra: ¿Una leyenda cómica?

Jorge: No. Una leyenda sobre México. Sobre nuestra historia. No tiene que ser cómica.

Beto: ¿Conoces una leyenda mexicana?

Sandra: Hay una leyenda sobre aquellos volcanes, pero no la conozco.

Guía: Yo conozco esa leyenda. ¿Cómo están?

Sandra: ¿De veras?

Guía: Claro. Había una vez un emperador azteca. Su hija, la princesa, se llamaba Ixtaccíhuatl.

Jorge: ¿Ixta— Ixtacc–? Ay, ¡qué difícil! ¿Por qué no se llamaba María?

ACTIVIDAD 7 - UNA LEYENDA

Level 2 Textbook p. 205

TXT CD 5, Track 4

Escucha la leyenda y contesta las preguntas.

Había una vez un emperador que vivía en un palacio grande con su hija hermosa, la princesa. La princesa estaba enamorada de un guerrero. Ellos querían casarse. Pero había un problema: la guerra. El guerrero era muy valiente y peleaba frecuentemente en batallas difíciles con enemigos fuertes. La princesa estaba muy triste. Lloraba y lloraba todos los días porque su héroe no estaba con ella. Iba a las montañas y les pedía ayuda a los dioses. Al terminar la guerra, el guerrero pasaba por las montañas, y allí encontró a la princesa. Los dos jóvenes se casaron, y luego el emperador, su hija, y el guerrero vivieron muy felices el resto de sus vidas.

PRONUNCIACIÓN

Level 2 Textbook p. 205

TXT CD 5, Track 5

El sonido **r** y **rr**

The Spanish **r** in the middle or at the end of a word is pronounced with a single tap of the tongue against the roof of your mouth. It sounds similar to the **d** of the English word *buddy*. Listen to and repeat these words.

empe**r**ador he**r**moso mo**r**ir

he**r**oína que**r**ido pe**r**o

The letter **r** at the beginning of a word and the double **rr** within a word is pronounced with several rapid taps of the tongue, or a trill. Listen and repeat.

gue**rr**a na**rr**ación piza**rr**ón

Ramón **r**ayas pe**rr**o

Los gue**rr**e**r**os no quieren pelea**r** en esta batalla.

El empe**r**ador está enamo**r**ado de la princesa **R**afaela.

TELEHISTORIA ESCENA 2

Level 2 Textbook p. 206

TXT CD 5, Track 6

Guía: La princesa Ixtaccíhuatl —bueno, mejor vamos a llamarla Ixta —era muy hermosa, y muchos hombres estaban enamorados de ella.

Sandra: Ixta, la heroína.

Guía: Popocatépetl —bueno, mejor vamos a llamarlo Popo.

Sandra: Ah...sí...¡los nombres de los volcanes!

Guía: ¡Exactamente! Popo era un guerrero valiente del emperador y un día llevó a su ejército a una guerra contra el enemigo.

Beto: ¿Cómo? ¿El emperador no era valiente? ¿Por qué no quería pelear él?

Guía: Él peleó en muchas batallas, pero ya era muy viejo. El emperador le dijo: «Para casarte con mi hija, debes ser valiente en la batalla y ganar la guerra».

Jorge: ¿Qué? ¿Y si no regresa?

Guía: Popocatépetl estaba enamorado de Ixtaccíhuatl, y ella estaba enamorada de él. Cuando Popo se fue a la batalla, la princesa Ixta estaba triste y lloró. Popo tenía que regresar para casarse con ella.

Jorge: ¡Ay! ¡Mujeres!

Audio Scripts

TELEHISTORIA COMPLETA

Level 2 Textbook p. 211

TXT CD 5, Track 7

Escena 1 Resumen Sandra, Jorge y Beto piensan en unas leyendas para su película. Un guía del parque empieza a contarles una leyenda sobre dos volcanes.

Escena 2 Resumen El guía habla de la princesa Ixtaccíhuatl y Popocatépetl. Popo quería casarse con Ixta, pero primero tenía que ganar la guerra para el padre de Ixta, el emperador.

Escena 3

Guía: Popo fue muy valiente y ganó la guerra. Pero otro guerrero tenía celos de Popo y regresó al palacio primero diciendo que Popo murió en la guerra.

Jorge: ¿Por qué hizo eso?

Guía: Porque él también estaba enamorado de la princesa.

Jorge: ¡Qué horror!

Guía: La princesa Ixta estaba tan triste que murió.

Jorge: ¡No puede ser!

Guía: Cuando Popo volvió al palacio encontró a la princesa. La llevó a la montaña más alta, donde los dioses transformaron al guerrero y a su princesa en dos volcanes, uno al lado del otro. Ixta está tranquila pero a menudo Popo se despierta y llora por ella. Y ésa es la leyenda de estos dos volcanes.

Sandra: ¡Qué hermosa leyenda!

Jorge: Creo que debemos hacer una leyenda cómica.

ACTIVIDAD 19 – INTEGRACIÓN

Level 2 Textbook p. 213

TXT CD 5, Track 8

Lee la pequeña historia y escucha el cuento. Describe lo que aprendes sobre Cortés y Moctezuma.

FUENTE 2

TXT CD 5, Track 9

Listen and take notes.

¿Quién era Quetzalcóatl?

¿Por qué pensó Moctezuma que Cortés era Quetzalcóatl?

¿Qué le dio Moctezuma a Cortés?

Los aztecas tenían una leyenda sobre Quetzalcóatl, un dios muy querido. Hacía muchos siglos él salió de México. Fue a una playa del Golfo de México, entró al mar y de allí subió, transformado en una luz de la mañana. Pero la leyenda contaba que Quetzalcóatl iba a regresar un día para ser el emperador de México. Como fue al mar, los aztecas pensaban que también iba a regresar del mar. Cuando Moctezuma II supo que unos hombres blancos y muy diferentes a los aztecas llegaron a Veracruz, el emperador pensó que por fin regresaba el dios Quetzalcóatl. Entonces Moctezuma le mandó a Hernán Cortés muchos regalos finos de joyas y de ropa, y lo invitó al palacio azteca.

LECTURA: UNA LEYENDA MAZATECA: EL FUEGO Y EL TLACUACHE

Level 2 Textbook pp. 214–215

TXT CD 5, Track 10

Hay muchas versiones de la leyenda sobre los orígenes del fuego. Ésta es la que cuentan los mazatecas que viven en la región norte de Oaxaca.

Hace muchos siglos, en el principio de los tiempos, las personas no conocían el fuego. Un día una piedra en llamas se cayó de una estrella. Todos tenían miedo de acercarse. Pero una mujer vieja se acercó y se llevó el fuego para su casa en una rama seca. Luego la piedra se apagó y los mazatecas se fueron a sus casas.

Pasaban los días y las personas que vivían cerca de la mujer vieja veían que el fuego era bueno y útil. La mujer lo usaba para cocinar la comida y para dar luz y calor. Pero ella no era muy simpática y no le gustaba compartir. Cuando los mazatecas le pedían un poco de fuego, siempre les decía que no.

Un día llegó un tlacuache inteligente y les dijo a los mazatecas que él podía traerles el fuego. Los mazatecas pensaban que eso era imposible. Si ellos no lo podían hacer, ¿cómo lo iba a hacer ese pequeño animal? Pero el tlacuache insistió en que él podía hacer y que les iba a dar el fuego a todos.

El tlacuache fue una noche a la casa de la vieja y vio que ella descansaba delante de un gran fuego.

—Buenas tardes, señora —dijo el tlacuache—. ¡Ay, que frío hace! Con su permiso, me gustaría estar un rato al lado del fuego.

La vieja sabía que sí hacía un frío terrible, y le permitió al tlacuache acercarse al fuego. En ese momento el tlacuache puso su cola directamente en el fuego y luego salió corriendo de la casa con la cola en llamas para darle el fuego a todas las personas de la región.

Y es por eso que los tlacuaches tienen las colas peladas.

REPASO: ACTIVIDAD 1 - LISTEN AND UNDERSTAND

Level 2 Textbook p. 218

TXT CD 5, Track 11

Escucha la descripción de las actividades de Gregorio y Andrés. Haz una copia de la tabla para escribir lo que quería hacer Gregorio o Andrés y lo que hicieron al final. Usa el imperfecto o el pretérito.

La semana pasada, mi amigo Gregorio y yo tuvimos que estudiar para un examen en la clase de ciencias el miércoles. Entonces el lunes Gregorio quería estudiar en la biblioteca y yo prefería estudiar en mi casa. Decidimos estudiar en mi casa.

Yo quería escuchar música, pero Gregorio no podía estudiar con música.

Entonces, no escuchamos música.

Gregorio prefería sentarse en la mesa de la cocina, pero yo quería estudiar en el sofá de la sala. Al final nos sentamos en la mesa de la cocina para estudiar.

Gregorio estudió con el libro y yo usé los apuntes que tomé en la clase.

Al fin, los dos sacamos una buena nota en el examen pero también aprendimos una cosa. Aprendimos que somos muy diferentes y es mejor no estudiar juntos. Entonces el sábado, en vez de estudiar, fuimos a jugar al fútbol.

Audio Scripts

INTEGRACIÓN: HABLAR

Level 2 Workbook p. 157

WB CD 2, Track 21

Escucha la continuación de la leyenda en el sitio web. Toma apuntes.

FUENTE 2

WB CD 2, Track 22

Ella respondió: «Eres muy simpático, pero no es posible. Mi padre es tu enemigo, el emperador.»

Entonces, el guerrero fue con ella al palacio para ver al emperador joven. El guerrero le dijo: «¡Esta guerra tiene que terminar! Quiero casarme con esta princesa, la hija de tu enemigo.»

Pero el emperador joven también estaba enamorado de la princesa y tenía celos del guerrero. Él dijo: «Querida princesa, yo soy trabajador y tengo mucho dinero. Debes vivir conmigo en este palacio grande y la guerra puede terminar.» La princesa no sabía qué hacer.

INTEGRACIÓN: ESCRIBIR

Level 2 Workbook p. 158

WB CD 2, Track 23

Escucha el mensaje telefónico de la maestra de la clase. Toma apuntes.

FUENTE 2

WB CD 2, Track 24

Hola, me llamo Soledad Vidal, la maestra de la clase. Gracias por llamarme para más información. Esta clase va a ser muy divertida. Primero les voy a leer parte de un libro que yo escribí. Después, vamos a escribir una leyenda. Luego vamos a tener una competencia para ver quién puede hacer el personaje más interesante. ¡Voy a traer premios! La clase está en el primer piso del Centro Académico, en la sala 8. Debes traer un cuaderno y una pluma contigo. ¡Hasta el lunes!

ESCUCHAR A, ACTIVIDAD 1

Level 2 Workbook p. 159

WB CD 2, Track 25

Escucha a Jaime. Luego, subraya las oraciones correspondientes a lo que dice.

Jaime: Me llamo Jaime y soy de México. Cuando era pequeño mi abuela siempre me contaba leyendas mexicanas. También las estudiaba en la escuela. Ahora soy profesor de español en Estados Unidos. Cada viernes le cuento leyendas a mi clase, pero el viernes pasado les pedí a los estudiantes unas leyendas contadas por ellos. ¡Las contaron muy bien!

ESCUCHAR A, ACTIVIDAD 2

Level 2 Workbook p. 159

WB CD 2, Track 26

Escucha la conversación de Graciela y Pablo. Luego, completa las oraciones.

Graciela: Pablo, me encantó la leyenda que contaste en la clase de español.

Pablo: ¿Sí? A mí me gustó mucho la que tú contaste. También me gustó la de los guerreros que peleaban en una batalla que no terminaba.

Graciela: Ésa fue fantástica. También me gustó la de la princesa que tenía celos del espejo.

Pablo: Ésa no me gustó mucho. La princesa siempre lloraba. Prefiero las historias con personajes valientes.

Graciela: Tal vez hay una sobre una princesa guerrera.

ESCUCHAR B, ACTIVIDAD 1

Level 2 Workbook p. 160

WB CD 2, Track 27

Escucha lo que dice Laura. Luego, pon en orden correcto los eventos de la leyenda que ella cuenta.

Laura: Mi abuela siempre me contaba leyendas de héroes, enemigos y personajes enamorados. Mi favorita era sobre una princesa que peleó en una batalla vestida como hombre. Los otros guerreros no sabían que era mujer, y ella peleó tan valientemente que el ejército azteca le ganó a su enemigo.

Cuando supieron los guerreros quién era, todos estuvieron enamorados de ella. Yo siempre quise ser una heroína como esa princesa.

ESCUCHAR B, ACTIVIDAD 2

Level 2 Workbook p. 160

WB CD 2, Track 28

Escucha a Jorge y toma apuntes. Luego, contesta las preguntas con oraciones completas.

Jorge: Mi hermana piensa que es una princesa. Eso es porque mi abuela siempre le contaba historias de princesas. El año pasado, compró un vestido de princesa y fue a la fiesta de una amiga vestida así. Yo no lo podía creer, pero todas sus amigas le dijeron que su vestido era el más bonito de la fiesta. Ahora, tiene que encontrar a un héroe y un palacio para completar su leyenda.

ESCUCHAR C, ACTIVIDAD 1

Level 2 Workbook p. 161

WB CD 2, Track 29

Escucha al señor Ortiz y toma apuntes. Luego, contesta las siguientes preguntas con oraciones completas.

Señor Ortiz: Mi nombre es Armando Ortiz, y en la escuela estudié mucho las leyendas de siglos pasados. Las leyendas eran una forma de contar la historia de sus países como las entendían ellos. Hablaban sobre sus dioses y sus héroes, y sobre sus plantas y animales. Originalmente contaban las leyendas oralmente porque todavía no sabían leer ni escribir. Pero un día empezaron a escribirlas, y así es como no están todas perdidas en el tiempo.

ESCUCHAR C, ACTIVIDAD 2

Level 2 Workbook p. 161

WB CD 2, Track 30

Escucha la conversación entre Claudia y Noemí. Toma apuntes. Luego, con tres oraciones completas cuenta de qué hablaba la leyenda que leyó Claudia.

Claudia: Noemí, ayer leí una leyenda muy hermosa.

Noemí: Hola, Claudia. ¿Una leyenda de princesas y héroes o una leyenda de guerreros y batallas?

Audio Scripts

Claudia: No, era una leyenda sobre unos amigos que estaban enamorados de la misma mujer. Los dos eran muy buenos amigos pero, cuando la mujer se casó con uno de ellos, el amigo más joven tenía muchos celos. Entonces, un día, cuando todos dormían, él salió para siempre.

Noemí: ¡Qué triste! En las leyendas siempre pasan esas cosas. Antes, yo leía muchas leyendas, pero ya no quiero saber más de peleas y celos.

Claudia: Pero tienes que entender que son sólo historias. Cuando yo era pequeña pensaba que todo lo que pasaba era cierto en las leyendas. El tiempo pasó y entendí que no era así. Todas las semanas leía leyendas. Todavía lo hago.

ASSESSMENT SCRIPTS
TEST CD 1

LESSON 1 TEST: ESCUCHAR
ACTIVIDAD A

Modified Assessment Book p. 119
On-level Assessment Book p. 160
Pre-AP Assessment Book p. 119
TEST CD 1, Track 21

Escucha el siguiente audio. Luego, completa la actividad A.

Luis: O, mi hermosa princesa Ixta. Ahora me voy a la guerra a pelear con el enemigo, pero al volver nos vamos a casar. Ya hablé con tu padre, nuestro emperador azteca.

Ana: Popo, tú eres mi héroe. Yo sé que vas a regresar por mí, pero si mueres, yo voy a morir también.

Luis: No debes decir eso, querida princesa. Nos vamos a ver otra vez después de ganar la batalla. Adiós, Ixta. Tienes que ser valiente. No me gusta verte llorar.

Ana: Adiós, Popo. Sé que el dios de la guerra va a estar contigo.

ACTIVIDAD B

Modified Assessment Book p. 119
On-level Assessment Book p. 160
Pre-AP Assessment Book p. 119
TEST CD 1, Track 22

Escucha el siguiente audio. Luego, completa la actividad B.

Carlos: Hija, tengo que hablar contigo. El guerrero heroico Chimali regresó hoy con su ejército. Estuvo aquí en el palacio y me contó que Popo murió en una terrible batalla.

Ana: ¡O, no! Creo que no. Chimali es el enemigo de Popo. Él no nos dice la verdad. Siempre tuvo celos de Popo.

Carlos: No, hija, es verdad. Popo murió. Chimali quiere casarse contigo ahora. Él está muy enamorado de ti.

Ana: Papá, yo no estoy enamorada de Chimali.

Carlos: Pero él es un guerrero valiente como Popo.

Ana: No me importa, papá. Me voy a la montaña a morir. Adiós, papá.

Carlos: ¡Pero, hija! ¡regresa! Los dioses te van a transformar en un volcán si no me escuchas. ¡Regresa!

HERITAGE LEARNERS SCRIPTS
HL CDs 1 & 3

INTEGRACIÓN HABLAR

Level 2 HL Workbook p. 159
HL CD 1, Track 25

Vas a escuchar el recado que Gisel Peña dejó a su amigo Abel. Toma notas.

FUENTE 2

HL CD 1, Track 26

Abel: Hola. Abel Suárez no está por el momento. Por favor deja un mensaje. Gracias.

Gisel: Hola Abel, habla Gisel. Te dejé un recado con tu mamá pero no sé si te lo pasó. La maestra de historia quiere que yo le haga un resumen de la leyenda que leyeron ayer en clase. Es trabajo de equipo, y como yo falté ayer a la escuela, no sé cuál es la leyenda. ¿Podrías por favor llamarme y darme la información? Por ejemplo: ¿Sobre qué era? ¿Quién la escribió? ¿Quiénes eran los personajes? Háblame pronto. Gracias.

INTEGRACIÓN: ESCRIBIR

Level 2 HL Workbook p. 160
HL CD 1, Track 27

Vas a escuchar un fragmento de un programa de radio para niños en que la poeta mexicana Lorena Villanueva habla de la leyenda «La Llorona».

FUENTE 2

HL CD 1, Track 28

Todos los países tienen sus leyendas. La leyenda de "La Llorona" es una de las más populares en México. Se cree que el mito original fue de los aztecas, quienes decían que una mujer vestida de blanco caminaba por las calles de Tenochtitlán llorando: "¡Ay, mi pobres hijos, ya pronto van a ser destruidos!". Con el tiempo, esta mujer se convirtió en una dama elegante que caminaba por las calles del México colonial, vestida de blanco llorando una gran pena. Su dolor era tanto que sus gritos se oían por toda la ciudad. Con el paso de los siglos la leyenda se convirtió en una historia favorita de las abuelas. La pobre llorona acabó siendo un madre que había perdido a sus hijos, una novia a quien le habían matado a su novio en la iglesia, una monja que se había vuelto loca porque no quería ser monja. Son muchas versiones de la misma leyenda.

LESSON 1 TEST: ESCUCHAR
ACTIVIDAD A

HL Assessment Book p. 125
HL CD 3, Track 21

Rodrigo, Gretchen, y el director están hablando de la obra de teatro que van a presentar. Escucha su conversación y luego contesta las preguntas usando oraciones completas.

Director: En la leyenda que vamos a presentar, Sebastián va a hacer el personaje del héroe, y Gretchen el personaje de la princesa.

Rodrigo: ¿Quién va a contar la leyenda?

Director: El narrador la va a contar, Rodrigo.

Gretchen: ¿Cómo empieza la leyenda? Quiero saber.

Rodrigo: Había una vez, en un palacio azteca, la Princesa Cloti...

Director: ¡Espera! Nos falta el emperador, que es el padre de la princesa.

Gretchen: Creo que Luis puede ser el emperador.

Director: Luis es un actor muy bueno, y puede hacer los dos personajes, el del emperador y el del enemigo.

Rodrigo: ¿Cómo termina esta leyenda? ¿El héroe se enamora de la princesa? ¿Hay una guerra?

Director: Finalmente, el héroe regresa y busca a la princesa para casarse con ella.

Audio Scripts

LESSON 1 TEST: ESCUCHAR ACTIVIDAD B

HL Assessment Book p. 125

HL CD 3, Track 22

Escucha la leyenda contada por la guía turística, y luego contesta las preguntas usando oraciones completas

Guía turística: México tiene muchas leyendas y una de mis favoritas es la de la montaña y el río. Hace muchos siglos, un emperador llamado Ticoti vivía con su hija, la princesa Alía en un palacio en la cima de una montaña.

Estudiante: ¿Cómo era la princesa?

Guía turística: La princesa era hermosa y simpática. Todos los jóvenes querían casarse con ella, pero Alía estaba enamorada del heroico guerrero Suamín. A Suamín lo llamaban "el guerrero valiente" porque peleaba contra los enemigos del emperador y siempre ganaba todas las batallas.

Un día, el guerrero Rolta fue al palacio del emperador y le dijo: "Quiero casarme con la princesa Alía." Entonces, el emperador le contestó: "Si quieres casarte con mi hija, tienes que pelear contra el guerrero Suamín. Si ganas la batalla, mi hija se va a casar contigo. Si pierdes, Suamín se va a casar con ella."

Estudiante: ¿Quién ganó la batalla? ¿Suamín o Rolta?

Guía turística: Rolta ganó la batalla. La princesa estaba tan triste que comenzó a llorar. Lloró tanto que la montaña se transformó en agua.

Estudiante: ¡Qué leyenda tan triste!

Audio Scripts

PRESENTACIÓN DE VOCABULARIO

Level 2 Textbook p. 222–223

TXT CD 5, Track 12

A. En México encontramos lo antiguo y lo moderno. Vemos lo antiguo en las ruinas de diferentes civilizaciones. Puedes conocer los templos, las pirámides y otros monumentos a los dioses de religiones antiguas.

B. En las excavaciones de las ruinas encontramos objetos de estas civilizaciones antiguas. Sabemos que ellos usaron herramientas y eran agricultores. Practicaban la agricultura y también cazaban animales para su comida. Usaban un calendario para contar los días del año.

C. El México moderno es avanzado. En la Ciudad de México puedes ver edificios nuevos, como este rascacielos o esta catedral.

D. ¿Cómo llegas a los lugares importantes? La mejor manera de conocer esta ciudad es visitar sus barrios y plazas. Camina por las avenidas o toma el metro o un autobús. Lo antiguo y lo moderno están delante de ti.

¡A RESPONDER!

Level 2 Textbook p. 223

TXT CD 5, Track 13

Escucha esta lista de palabras. Levanta la mano derecha si lo encuentras en una ruina. Levanta la mano izquierda si lo encuentras en una ciudad moderna.

1. una estatua de una diosa tolteca
2. una pirámide
3. un rascacielos
4. un semáforo
5. el calendario antiguo
6. la acera
7. una cuadra de edificios modernos

TELEHISTORIA ESCENA 1

Level 2 Textbook p. 225

TXT CD 5, Track 14

Beto: Perdón, ¿está el cine Diana en este barrio?

Mujer: Sí. Cerca de ese rascacielos.

Jorge: ¿Cómo llegamos allí? ¿Seguimos derecho?

Mujer: Deben doblar a la izquierda y caminar dos cuadras. Después doblan a la derecha y van hasta el siguiente semáforo. El cine está en la esquina. Pero ¿está cerrado?

Sandra: No vamos al cine, vamos a la parada de autobuses frente al cine. Vamos para Tula.

Mujer: ¡A Tula! ¿A ver las ruinas? ¿Es para el colegio?

Jorge: No, no. Hace unos días que filmamos una película sobre leyendas mexicanas, y ahora queremos saber más sobre la historia de México.

Mujer: ¡Fantástico! ¿A qué hora sale el autobús?

Sandra: Muy pronto. ¡Gracias! ¡A la izquierda!

ACTIVIDAD 6 - ¿ADÓNDE FUE?

Level 2 Textbook p. 228

TXT CD 5, Track 15

¿Puedes encontrar los lugares que Luisa visitó en un barrio antiguo de la Ciudad de México? Mientras escuchas, dobla a la izquierda o la derecha según el punto de vista de Luisa. Escribe la letra del edificio o del lugar que Luisa visitó en cada paso.

1. Empecé mi excursión del Centro Histórico en el Gran Hotel. Salí del hotel, crucé la calle Monte de Piedad y llegué a la plaza.

2. Seguí derecho hasta el centro de la plaza y luego doblé a la izquierda. Crucé la plaza y llegué frente a un edificio grande. Crucé la calle y entré al edificio.

3. Después de tomar fotos de la escultura en la catedral, salí a la calle otra vez. De la puerta de la catedral, doblé a la izquierda y comencé a caminar hasta llegar a la esquina de la calle República de Argentina. En la esquina doblé a la izquierda y caminé una cuadra. Crucé la calle y allí llegué a las ruinas.

4. Después de ver las ruinas y tomar fotos, fui al museo al lado. El museo está en la esquina de las calles Justo Sierra y Carmen.

5. Decidí almorzar. Del museo seguí por la calle Justo Sierra hasta llegar a la calle Monte de Piedad. Doblé a la izquierda y caminé dos cuadras. En la segunda cuadra a la derecha vi un lugar bonito y allí almorcé.

6. Pagué la cuenta del almuerzo y decidí caminar un poco. Salí otra vez a la calle Monte de Piedad y caminé a la derecha. Pasé tres cuadras y doblé a la derecha. Caminé tres cuadras y doblé otra vez a la derecha. Caminé otras tres cuadras y en la esquina de la tercera cuadra encontré este rascacielos muy conocido.

TELEHISTORIA ESCENA 2

Level 2 Textbook p. 230

TXT CD 5, Track 16

Guía Turística: ¡Bienvenidos a Tula! Hace muchos siglos—antes de los aztecas—una civilización muy antigua, los toltecas, construyó estas pirámides y monumentos.

Beto: ¡Es una estatua de mi tío!

Sandra: ¡Sshh!

Guía Turística: No sabemos mucho sobre la gente de Tula. Sabemos que eran grandes militares, algunos cazaban y otros eran agricultores. Hacían cerámica y esculturas de dioses, como ésta.

Jorge: No está muy alegre, ¿verdad?

Sandra: No, creo que no almorzó.

Jorge: O que sacó una mala nota en la clase de matemáticas.

Beto: O que pagó demasiado por ese sombrero.

Audio Scripts

PRONUNCIACIÓN

Level 2 Textbook p. 231

TXT CD 5, Track 17

El sonido /s/

The Spanish *s* is pronounced like the *s* of the English word *sell*. The Spanish *c* (before *e* and *i*) and *z* make this same sound. Listen and repeat.

s	Sandra	sobre
z	azteca	cazar
ce	cero	acera
ci	ciudad	edificio

Los aztecas eran una civilización avanzada.

La princesa cruzó el río a la izquierda en busca de su palacio.

Note that in central and northern Spain, the letters *c* (before *e* and *i*) and *z* are pronounced like the *th* of the English word *think*.

z	azteca	cazar
ce	cero	acera
ci	ciudad	edificio

Los aztecas eran una civilización avanzada.

La princesa cruzó el río a la izquierda en busca de su palacio.

TELEHISTORIA COMPLETA

Level 2 Textbook p. 235

TXT CD 5, Track 18

Narrator: *Escena 1 Resumen* Beto, Jorge y Sandra buscan la parada de autobuses para ir a Tula. Una mujer les dice cómo llegar. Ellos le dicen a la mujer por qué quieren ir a Tula.

Escena 2 Resumen Una guía turística les cuenta la historia de Tula a los jóvenes. Habla de la cultura de los toltecas. Los jóvenes miran una estatua de un dios tolteca.

Escena 3

Beto: Tenemos que regresar. Debemos estar en casa a las seis.

Sandra: ¿Dónde está Jorge? Estaba aquí cuando fui a comprar un refresco.

Beto: Allí está.

Jorge: ¡Eh! Encontré algo: ¡un objeto!

Beto: ¿Qué es? ¿Una herramienta antigua? ¿Un tesoro?

Sandra: ¿Dónde lo encontraste?

Jorge: Pues, yo estaba allí. Quería tomar una foto del templo pero no podía verlo bien desde aquí. Cuando crucé la plaza, encontré el objeto.

Guía: Ya pude limpiarlo un poco. Es de una civilización muy avanzada.

Jorge: ¿De verdad?

Guía: Sí, sí, dice: «Hecho en México, 2006».

ACTIVIDAD 18 – INTEGRACIÓN

Level 2 Textbook p. 237

TXT CD 5, Track 19

Mira el mapa y escucha a la guía. Luego describe tu visita al museo, lo que viste y lo que aprendiste.

ACTIVIDAD 18 – INTEGRACIÓN, FUENTE 2

TXT CD 5, Track 20

Listen and take notes.

¿Qué quiere decir «Mexica»?

¿Dónde queda el Templo Mayor? ¿Qué objetos encontraron allí?

Ahora estamos en la Sala Mexica. «Mexica» es otro nombre para «azteca»; «mexica» era el nombre que ellos usaban. Los aztecas, o mexicas, construyeron su capital aquí hace muchos siglos. Hoy las ruinas del antiguo Templo Mayor de los aztecas quedan en el centro de la ciudad de México moderna. Durante una excavación del Templo Mayor encontraron este objeto grande, la Piedra del Sol, también conocida como el Calendario Azteca. Antes estaba pintada de rojo y amarillo. Allí también encontraron esa estatua grande de la diosa Coatlicue que ves al otro lado de la sala. Ahora cruza la sala para verla de cerca.

LECTURA CULTURAL: LOS ZAPOTECAS Y LOS OTAVALEÑOS

Level 2 Textbook pp. 238–239

TXT CD 5, Track 21

La región de Oaxaca tiene base sobre antiguas civilizaciones como la zapoteca. Monte Albán, la antigua capital zapoteca, es una zona de ruinas de más de 1.300 años. Allí hay un campo de pelota, una gran plaza, un palacio, varios templos y otros edificios y estructuras. Todavía hoy, la presencia de los zapotecas es muy fuerte en Oaxaca. Hoy continúan la tradición de trabajo en cerámica con técnicas tradicionales: usan, por ejemplo, decoraciones zapotecas auténticas. También, todos los años, los oaxaqueños celebran la Guelaguetza, una ceremonia indígena ancestral. La palabra «guelaguetza» es zapoteca y quiere decir «regalo».

El pasado y el presente de los otavaleños es parte esencial del Ecuador moderno. Los indígenas de Otavalo vivían en Ecuador antes del imperio inca y su civilización prospera magníficamente en el presente. Hoy en día, los otavaleños están muy bien organizados comercialmente. Producen artículos de ropa y de decoración con tejidos de colores únicos. Venden estos productos en Ecuador, pero también por otros países de Latinoamérica, Estados Unidos y Europa. Se consideran internacionalmente un modelo para el progreso económico de los pueblos. También, todavía celebran ceremonias ancestrales. Todos los años, al final del verano, celebran la fiesta del Yamor, en honor a la madre tierra.

REPASO: ACTIVIDAD 1 - LISTEN AND UNDERSTAND

Level 2 Textbook p. 242

TXT CD 5, Track 22

Rosario describe una lección sobre civilizaciones antiguas. Escucha y luego combina frases de las columnas para describir lo que pasó.

Rosario: El mes pasado mi amiga Catarina y yo hicimos un proyecto sobre civilizaciones antiguas para la clase de historia. Primero leímos un libro sobre las ruinas en México. Yo no sabía que las civilizaciones antiguas de México eran tan avanzadas. Luego, construimos dos pirámides con la información que aprendimos y escribimos un resumen. La maestra pensó que las pirámides eran excelentes. Ella también leyó el resumen y le gustó mucho.

Para la semana siguiente, yo leí otro libro sobre la agricultura y la vida diaria de los toltecas y Catarina leyó un libro sobre los templos religiosos en Tula. Entonces, yo construí un modelo de una excavación y ella hizo una

Audio Scripts

estatua como las de los toltecas. Para terminar el proyecto, escribimos un reporte sobre todo lo que aprendimos haciendo el proyecto y la maestra lo leyó. Fue una experiencia muy interesante.

COMPARACIÓN CULTURAL: LO ANTIGUO Y LO MODERNO EN MI CUIDAD.

Level 2 Textbook pp. 244–245

TXT CD 5, Track 23

Nicaragua, Martín

¡Saludos desde Nicaragua! Soy Martín y vivo en Granada. Ésta es la ciudad colonial más antigua construida en América. Todavía puedes ver edificios y catedrales que tienen más de 300 años. Las puertas y las ventanas de las casas tienen diseños coloniales típicos. Muchas personas que viven aquí prefieren viajar por la ciudad en coches tirados por caballos como lo hacían antes. ¡A veces pienso que estoy viviendo en otro siglo!

Ecuador, Elena

¿Qué tal? Me llamo Elena y vivo en Quito, una ciudad de contrastes. En el barrio histórico, los templos, edificios y monumentos antiguos me dan una idea de cómo era la ciudad en el pasado. ¡Me encanta! Pero también me gusta caminar por el área moderna y admirar los rascacielos grandes.

México, Raúl

¡Hola! Soy Raúl. Vivo en Cancún, México, muy cerca de la playa. Vivir aquí es muy interesante. Es un lugar moderno pero con mucha historia. Hace muchos siglos los mayas vivieron aquí y construyeron palacios y templos. Es posible ver las ruinas aquí, pero el edificio que me gusta más es este hotel moderno inspirado en las pirámides mayas. ¡Qué original!

REPASO INCLUSIVO: ACTIVIDAD 1 LISTEN, UNDERSTAND, AND COMPARE

Level 2 Textbook p. 248

TXT CD 5, Track 24

Listen to this guide give a tour of Mexico City's Zócalo and then answer the following questions.

Guía: Aquí estamos en el Zócalo, la plaza más grande de las Américas. Otro nombre para el Zócalo es La Plaza de la Constitución. Vamos a ir primero al Palacio Nacional. El presidente vive allí. Dentro del palacio, hay unos murales hermosos del artista famoso Diego Rivera. Frente al Palacio Nacional, al otro lado del Zócalo, queda el Gran Hotel. Este hotel tiene más de cien habitaciones y es muy popular para los turistas. Está en un buen lugar, con vistas excelentes de la plaza.

A la izquierda del Palacio Nacional pueden encontrar las ruinas del Templo Mayor. Fue una pirámide de los aztecas que los trabajadores encontraron durante la excavación. También hay otros edificios aztecas que encontraron en la excavación. Al lado de las ruinas queda el Museo del Templo Mayor. En el museo puedes ver más herramientas y objetos antiguos.

Delante del Templo Mayor tenemos la Catedral Metropolitana. Vamos a cruzar la plaza y la calle para entrar a esta catedral ahora. La Catedral Metropolitana es muy antigua y es la iglesia más grande en Centroamérica. Ahora vamos a entrar para ver el interior.

WORKBOOK SCRIPTS
WB CD 2

INTEGRACIÓN: HABLAR

Level 2 Workbook p. 180

WB CD 2, Track 31

Escucha el mensaje sobre la nueva película «Ciudades y rascacielos» y toma apuntes.

FUENTE 2

WB CD 2, Track 32

¡Gracias por llamar a Cine México! Recomendamos la nueva película «Ciudades y rascacielos», una película sobre el hombre moderno y sus edificios modernos. Desde los tiempos antiguos, el hombre construyó. Sigue haciéndolo hoy con herramientas avanzadas. En las ciudades grandes vemos rascacielos más y más altos. El hombre moderno puede viajar a todas las ciudades en avión para verlos. En esta película puedes hacer un viaje también a estas ciudades grandes para ver muchos rascacielos y otros edificios modernos. ¡Ven a verla hoy!

INTEGRACIÓN: ESCRIBIR

Level 2 Workbook p. 181

WB CD 2, Track 33

Escucha un mensaje telefónico de Lola, la amiga de Mariela. Toma apuntes.

FUENTE 2

WB CD 2, Track 34

Hola, Mariela. Habla Lola. Bueno, hay muchas cosas para ver y hacer en la Ciudad de México y la región. No puedes hacer todo, pero te recomiendo el Templo Mayor, ¡ruinas antiguas en el centro de la ciudad¡ Pero sé que te gustan los edificios modernos también, y cerca del Parque Alameda hay un hotel que es un rascacielos. También hay que ver el Monumento a la Independencia, un monumento muy famoso y alto con una estatua bella. Y debes ir al Museo Nacional de Antropología—tiene un calendario azteca y otros objetos interesantes. Si tienes tiempo para una excursión, debes ir a la ciudad de Puebla. Tiene muchas iglesias históricas y es un buen lugar para comprar cerámicas. Pero el viaje por autobús dura dos horas. ¡Hasta luego!

ESCUCHAR A, ACTIVIDAD 1

Level 2 Workbook p. 182

WB CD 2, Track 35

Escucha a Carolina. Luego, lee cada oración y contesta **cierto** o **falso**.

Mi familia y yo fuimos el año pasado a visitar las ruinas de una civilización antigua. Mi amiga Francesca vino con nosotros. Quisimos ver las pinturas muy antiguas dentro de la tumba de un emperador pero no pudimos entrar a verlas. Yo busqué unas herramientas en el sitio de una excavación, y Francesca sacó los objetos para dar a la guía. ¡Nos dijo que debemos ser arqueólogas!

ESCUCHAR A, ACTIVIDAD 2

Level 2 Workbook p. 182

WB CD 2, Track 36

Escucha a Raúl. Luego, completa las siguientes oraciones.

Hoy conté en la clase de historia de una excursión que hice el año pasado

Audio Scripts

a unas ruinas toltecas. Llegué a una excavación donde las personas sacaban herramientas antiguas. Yo pude participar, y saqué unos objetos interesantes. No los traje a clase, porque tuvimos que dejarlos todos allí.

ESCUCHAR B, ACTIVIDAD 1

Level 2 Workbook p. 183

WB CD 2, Track 37

Escucha la conversación entre Lorenzo y Carla. Luego, marca con una cruz las cosas que hizo Lorenzo.

Lorenzo: Hola, Carla. ¿Sabías que el año pasado visité unas ruinas con mi padre? Él fue a estudiar la civilización azteca. Conocí cosas muy interesantes.

Carla: ¡Qué bueno! ¿Qué hicieron?

Lorenzo: Bueno, mi papá me dijo cómo los aztecas construyeron las pirámides. Él me llevó a visitar una excavación. Después quisimos ir a la ciudad. Allí también hay cosas maravillosas. Un día almorcé en un buen restaurante y empecé a caminar por las plazas y avenidas.

Carla: ¿Y no te perdiste?

Lorenzo: No. Las personas me dijeron cómo llegar a todos los lugares. ¡Pero mi papá sí!

ESCUCHAR B, ACTIVIDAD 2

Level 2 Workbook p. 183

WB CD 2, Track 38

Escucha a Cristina. Luego, contesta las preguntas con oraciones completas.

Hola, soy Cristina López y soy una estudiante de historia. Acabo de regresar de mi viaje a México. Fui desde enero hasta julio para conocer la civilización tolteca. Cuando llegué a la ciudad, quise ir rápidamente a las ruinas. No sabía cómo llegar. Entonces una señora dijo que había un autobús que me podía llevar hasta allí. Estuve en las ruinas antiguas por un tiempo y luego vine a la ciudad para visitar los museos. Traje unas fotos, si quieres verlas.

ESCUCHAR C, ACTIVIDAD 1

Level 2 Workbook p. 184

WB CD 2, Track 39

Escucha la conversación entre Lucía y Fernando. Toma apuntes. Luego, completa las siguientes oraciones.

Lucía: ¡Hola, Fernando! No sabes qué libro tan interesante terminé ayer.

Fernando: ¡Hola, Lucía! ¿Un libro sobre qué?

Lucía: Es un libro que me recomendó mi mamá. Ella lo leyó ya varias veces y me dejó leerlo. Habla de las religiones de las civilizaciones antiguas.

Fernando: ¡Qué interesante! Yo no sé nada sobre eso.

Lucía: Bueno, te cuento. Las religiones de esas civilizaciones tenían muchos dioses.

Fernando: ¿Muchos dioses?

Lucía: Sí. Y las personas construyeron templos y pirámides para ellos. El libro es interesante porque habla de las conexiones entre las religiones de diferentes civilizaciones.

Fernando: La religión es una característica de las culturas de todos los tiempos, desde los antiguos hasta los modernos.

ESCUCHAR C, ACTIVIDAD 2

Level 2 Workbook p. 184

WB CD 2, Track 40

Escucha a Sonia y toma apuntes. Luego, contesta las siguientes preguntas con oraciones completas.

Ayer estuve en una librería y vi un libro muy interesante sobre la civilización tolteca. Tenía muchas fotos de los monumentos que construyeron y mucha información sobre su cultura avanzada. Le pregunté a la vendedora cuánto costaba y me dijo que 500 pesos. ¡No quise pagar tanto! Entonces salí, doblé a la derecha, crucé la avenida y llegué a la Biblioteca Nacional. Allí encontré el libro y lo traje a casa. ¡Y no pagué nada!

ASSESSMENT SCRIPTS
TEST CD 1

LESSON 2 TEST: ESCUCHAR ACTIVIDAD A

Modified Assessment Book p. 131

On-level Assessment Book p. 177

Pre-AP Assessment Book p. 131

TEST CD 1, Track 23

Escucha el siguiente audio. Luego, completa la actividad A.

La civilización maya fue una de las civilizaciones más avanzadas del México antiguo. Las ruinas que vemos en Yucatán y Guatemala nos dicen que los mayas tuvieron una cultura muy avanzada en las artes y en las ciencias. Ellos pudieron construir muchas pirámides, templos y palacios de piedra. Trabajaron la piedra usando herramientas para hacer sus estatuas y esculturas de sus dioses. Fueron buenos agricultores y también cazaron animales para comer. También estudiaron la astronomía y las matemáticas y tuvieron un calendario de 365 días.

ACTIVIDAD B

Modified Assessment Book p. 131

On-level Assessment Book p. 177

Pre-AP Assessment Book p. 131

TEST CD 1, Track 24

Escucha el siguiente audio. Luego, completa la actividad B.

Esta pirámide maya se llama El Castillo y es la pirámide más grande de Chichén-Itzá. Está dedicada a Kukulcán, un dios muy importante para la cultura maya. Se llamó Quetzalcóatl entre los toltecas y los aztecas. Es una pirámide de 78 pies de alto. En las excavaciones de El Castillo encontramos que en el interior había otra pirámide más pequeña. Primero pensamos que el Castillo era una tumba de un emperador tolteca o maya, pero después vimos que era un monumento para Kukulcán. Bien, vamos a subir.

UNIT 4 TEST: ESCUCHAR ACTIVIDAD A

Modified Assessment Book p. 143

On-level Assessment Book p. 189

Pre-AP Assessment Book p. 143

TEST CD 1, Track 25

Escucha el siguiente audio. Luego, completa la actividad A.

Turista: Perdón, ¿está el Gran Hotel lejos de aquí?

Carlos: No, el hotel está cerca. Está al lado del Zócalo, la plaza principal.

Turista: ¿Cómo llego allí?

Carlos: No es muy difícil. Debe seguir derecho por esta avenida, dos cuadras,

Audio Scripts

hasta llegar a la calle Corregidora. Allí hay un semáforo. En esa esquina hay que doblar a la derecha y caminar tres cuadras hasta llegar a un edificio muy grande, el Palacio Presidencial. Tiene que cruzar el Zócalo y entonces va a ver su hotel a la derecha.

Turista: Voy a repetirlo: camino dos cuadras por esta avenida. En la esquina, donde hay un semáforo, doblo a la derecha. Sigo tres cuadras. Después de cruzar el Zócalo—la plaza—mi hotel está a la derecha.

Carlos: ¡Perfecto!

Turista: Gracias. Adiós.

ACTIVIDAD B

Modified Assessment Book p. 143

On-level Assessment Book p. 189

Pre-AP Assessment Book p. 143

TEST CD 1, Track 26

Escucha el siguiente audio. Luego, completa la actividad B.

Ana: Profesor Gómez, ¿quién era Huitzi... Huitzilo...?

Profesor: ¿Hui-tzi-lo-poch-tli? Él era el dios más importante de los aztecas....

Ana: Oh, ¿fue el dios que les dijo a los aztecas dónde debían construir su ciudad?

Profesor: ¡Correcto! Él era el dios del sol y de la guerra. En las leyendas aztecas, los guerreros que murieron en batalla fueron a servirlo en su palacio.

Ana: Entonces, ¿es la cara que pusieron en el centro del Calendario Azteca?

Profesor: No sabemos, pero unos piensan que sí. También había otro dios del sol, más viejo que Huitzilopochtli, y unos piensan que es él. Otros dicen que es el dios del centro del universo.

MIDTERM EXAM
ESCUCHAR, ACTIVIDAD A

Modified Assessment Book p. 155

On-level Assessment Book p. 201

Pre-AP Assessment Book p. 155

TEST CD 1, Track 27

Escucha el siguiente audio. Luego, completa la actividad A.

Ayer tuve un día horrible y quiero contarles lo que me pasó. Como siempre, me desperté a las 6:00 pero no me levanté hasta las 6:15. Primero me duché y me lavé el pelo con champú. Luego me sequé con la toalla, me puse desodorante y me afeité. Entonces me puse la ropa de la escuela y bajé a desayunar. Mis padres y mi hermana Elena no estaban en la cocina. Pensé que todavía dormían. Después del desayuno subí a mi cuarto, me cepillé los dientes en el baño y me puse un suéter porque hacía frío. Tomé mis libros y por fin salí para la escuela muy contento. Como era temprano y no tenía prisa, decidí caminar y no tomé el autobús. El día estaba muy bonito. Cuando llegué a la escuela, vi que no estaba abierta. ¡Era sábado! ¡Qué día!

ESCUCHAR, ACTIVIDAD B

Modified Assessment Book p. 155

On-level Assessment Book p. 201

Pre-AP Assessment Book p. 105

TEST CD 1, Track 28

Escucha el siguiente audio. Luego, completa la actividad B.

Eloísa: Elena, ¿adónde fuiste para las vacaciones de invierno?

Elena: Fui a Puerto Rico con mis padres a visitar a mi abuela que vive en San Juan. Pasamos una semana con ella. Fue muy divertido.

Eloísa: ¿Qué hiciste?

Elena: Fui a la playa con mis padres. Un día hicimos una excursión al Yunque y dimos caminatas. Otro día monté a caballo con mis primos y un domingo fui a pescar con mi tío Nicolás y su hijo Raúl. Tomé muchas fotos durante todo el viaje. Me gustó mucho ir a los mercados con mi prima Ana y regatear. Hay muchas artesanías bonitas y muchas cosas hechas a mano. Mira, allí me compré estos aretes de oro y este anillo de plata. ¿Te gustan?

Eloísa: ¡Qué bellos! ¡Fueron muy caros?

Elena: No, muy baratos porque regateé en el mercado. Y en una zapatería compré estas sandalias de cuero.

Eloísa: Me encantan. Bueno, me parece que tu viaje a Puerto Rico fue muy divertido.

HERITAGE LEARNER SCRIPTS
HL CDs 1 & 3

INTEGRACIÓN: HABLAR

Level 2 HL Workbook p. 182

HL CD 1, Track 29

Vas a escuchar el recado que dejó Amador Muñoz a su familia. Toma notas.

FUENTE 2

HL CD 1, Track 30

Señora: Hola. No estamos en casa por el momento. Por favor deje un mensaje. Gracias.

Señor Múñoz: Sólo llamo para decirles que estoy bien, que la estamos pasando muy bien en la Ciudad de México. Ayer fuimos a ver las ruinas de un templo y aprendimos mucho sobre los antiguos mexicas. En el histórico centro de la ciudad visitamos el palacio de gobierno y vimos a unos danzantes aztecas que se llaman matachines. Llevan vestimenta azteca con penacho de plumas y cascabeles en los tobillos. La danza me pareció muy llena de vida y energía. También visitamos unos jardines flotantes llenos de flores.

INTEGRACIÓN: ESCRIBIR

Level 2 HL Workbook p. 183

HL CD 1, Track 31

Vas a escuchar un anuncio de radio que habla sobre la Ciudad de México. Toma notas.

FUENTE 2

HL CD 1, Track 32

Woman: ¿Por qué visitar la Ciudad de México? Porque, ¿no le gustaría ver el encuentro de dos civilizaciones y cómo se mezclaron dos culturas para producir una bella e interesantísima ciudad moderna?

En la Ciudad de México los sitios históricos, como por ejemplo las excavaciones de los templos antiguos, permiten al turista ver los recuerdos de una de las civilizaciones antiguas más interesantes y avanzadas. México es un país lleno de magia y de sorpresas. Hay que visitar sus museos, edificios, y también sus grandes avenidas y sus rascacielos modernos. ¿Y qué decir de la cocina mexicana? Solamente esto: Prepárese a comer, amigo, porque los mexicanos saben cocinar.

Audio Scripts

LESSON 2 TEST: ESCUCHAR ACTIVIDAD A

HL Assessment Book p. 137

HL CD 3, Track 23

Escucha la conversación entre Carmen y Raquel, y luego contesta las preguntas usando oraciones completas.

Carmen: Hola. ¿Quién habla?

Raquel: ¿Cómo estás, Carmen? Soy yo, Raquel. Quiero visitar el Museo de Antropología. ¿Sabes como llego?

Carmen: Sí. ¿Dónde estás?

Raquel: Estoy en el centro de la ciudad. Entre la avenida Las Américas y la calle 37.

Carmen: Primero, debes caminar dos cuadras hacia la calle Lorca. Luego, dobla a la derecha en la calle Presidente. Después, debes seguir derecho hasta que llegues al rascacielos El Sol.

Raquel: ¿Cómo es el rascacielos?

Carmen: Es un edificio moderno y muy alto. Tiene 50 pisos.

Raquel: ¿Y qué hago después? ¿Sigo derecho?

Carmen: No, no. Frente al rascacielos se encuentra el Museo de Antropología. Es un edificio que tiene una estatua de un dios azteca en la plaza. No te puedes perder.

Raquel: Después de ir al museo, quiero visitar el centro comercial. ¿Sabes dónde queda?

Carmen: No estoy segura, pero ve a la oficina de turismo que está al lado del museo y pide información.

Raquel: Gracias, Carmen.

Carmen: De nada.

LESSON 2 TEST: ESCUCHAR ACTIVIDAD B

HL Assessment Book p. 137

HL CD 3, Track 24

Escucha la carta que le escribió Gabriela a Diana, y luego contesta las preguntas usando oraciones completas.

Yo me llamo Gabriela, y este año hice un viaje a México. El primer día, conocí la capital, Distrito Federal. Visité rascacielos y edificios modernos. También caminé por los barrios y plazas de la ciudad. Quería ir a un centro comercial, pero no sabía cómo llegar. Entonces, le pregunté a un joven, y me dijo que había un centro comercial muy cerca del Museo Nacional.

Después fui a las ruinas toltecas para ver los templos y pirámides que estas civilizaciones construyeron hace muchos siglos. Los toltecas hacían monumentos a los dioses de religiones antiguas. Usaban herramientas y practicaban la agricultura. También cazaban animales y usaban el calendario para contar los días del año. Tenían una civilización muy avanzada.

Tomé muchas fotos de mi viaje. Y aprendí que en México puedes disfrutar de lo antiguo y lo moderno.

UNIT 4 TEST: ESCUCHAR ACTIVIDAD A

HL Assessment Book p. 149

HL CD 3, Track 25

Escucha la conversación entre Luis y Carmen, y luego contesta las preguntas usando oraciones completas.

Luis: No me gustan las historias sobre leyendas antiguas. Siempre hablan de guerreros, enemigos, guerras. Yo prefiero las historias donde se combina lo antiguo y lo moderno, como en la película "Quinientos Años".

Carmen: ¿De qué hablas?

Luis: Es una película muy cómica sobre un emperador azteca que sale de su tumba y regresa a la Ciudad de México, después de 500 años, para ver cómo es la civilización de hoy. Primero, visitó Distrito Federal y vio rascacielos, edificios modernos y centros comerciales. Después caminó por las calles y avenidas de la ciudad. Tenía hambre, pero no tenía dinero para ir a un restaurante. Entonces...

Carmen: ¿Qué hizo?

Luis: Le preguntó a una joven que estaba en una plaza: «Donde está la comida?» Pero la joven no le entendió.

Carmen: ¿Por qué?

Luis: El emperador no hablaba español. Hablaba un idioma azteca que ella no conocía. Entonces, la joven vio que el emperador tenía un collar de oro en el cuello: el mismo collar que tenía la escultura del Museo de Antropología. Entonces la joven lo llevó hasta una escultura que tenía el mensaje: «En honor a uno de los emperadores más heróicos de México.» Cuando el emperador la vió, comenzó a llorar de emoción.

Carmen: ¡Oh!

Luis: Cuando ella lo vio llorando, pensó que el emperador tenía hambre, así que le dijo: «Voy a llevarlo a un restaurante. ¿Le gustan los tamales?»

Carmen: Me parece que esa película es muy cómica.

UNIT 4 TEST: ESCUCHAR ACTIVIDAD B

HL Assessment Book p. 149

HL CD 3, Track 26

Escucha la conversación entre Alberto y una señora que encuentra en la calle. Después completa la actividad B.

Alberto: Disculpe, señora, no soy de la ciudad y estoy perdido. ¿Puede decirme dónde queda la plaza central?

Señora: Sí, con mucho gusto. Siga derecho por esta calle hasta la esquina del semáforo. Cruce la avenida y doble a la izquierda. Va a ver unos rascacielos. Siga dos cuadras más y luego doble a la derecha.

Alberto: ¿Y allí está la plaza?

Señora: No, allí va a ver unos edificios altos y un monumento a la libertad. La plaza esta cerca. Solamente siga caminando tres cuadras más allá del monumento y llegará a la plaza. Tiene varios edificios coloniales y una gran estatua en el centro.

Alberto: Me parece un poco lejos.

Señora: No, no está lejos. Está a pocas cuadras de aquí, pero si prefiere, puede tomar un taxi o un autobús.

Alberto: Hm… Creo que no. Prefiero caminar.

HL MIDTERM EXAM: ACTIVIDAD A

HL Assessment Book p. 161

HL CD 3, Track 27

Escucha una conversación entre Sofía y Carlos. Luego selecciona la mejor opción para completar la información o responder a las preguntas.

Sofía: Carlos, ¿estás contento de volver a casa?

Carlos: Sí Sofía; la verdad es que estas vacaciones fueron muy largas.

Sofía: Yo no diría que fueron largas sino agitadas...¡cuatro países en siete días!

Carlos: ¡Ay! ¡Me acabo de acordar! ¿Alguien sabe dónde está la mola panameña que le compramos a mi

Audio Scripts

mamá? Ella fue muy enfática cuando le dijimos que se la íbamos a comprar.

Sofía: Todas las molas están dentro de tu mochila.

Carlos: Eso quiere decir que en la mía están las artesanías y cerámicas.

Sofía: Exacto. Como eres el más cuidadoso del grupo, preferimos que seas tú quien las lleves porque estamos seguros de que no se van a romper.

Carlos: Vamos, ya es la hora de irnos. ¿Tienen todos sus pasaportes y boletos listos?

HL MIDTERM EXAM: ACTIVIDAD B

HL Assessment Book p. 161

HL CD 3, Track 28

Escucha la lectura de una carta que Irene le mandó a su prima Elena. Luego escoge las mejores respuestas.

Querida Elena:

Mi mamá acaba de anunciar que vas a pasar una semana en marzo con nosotros. Tuve que escribirte inmediatamente para decirte que estoy muy contenta. Tres años sin verte es demasiado tiempo. Vamos a pasar mucho tiempo en la playa. Ya sé que te encanta jugar en las olas, buscar caracoles y relajarte debajo de un palmar. También sé que vives en una ciudad lejos de un océano, donde hace mucho frío en marzo. Debes protegerte bien del sol. Pero no traigas loción protectora ni sombrilla. Puedes usar las nuestras. No te olvides de traer sandalias porque la arena puede quemarte los pies.

Desafortunadamente faltan cuatro semanas hasta tu llegada. Tengo muchísimas ganas de verte.

Con mucho cariño,

tu prima Irene

Map/Culture Activities *México*

1 Estas frases describen diferentes lugares en México. Complétalas con los nombres
de los lugares que están en la caja. Después localiza (*locate*) los lugares en el mapa y
escribe el número de la frase de abajo que corresponde al lugar.

Veracruz	Oaxaca	Ciudad de México	Ciudad Juárez	Zócalo

1. Si quieres ver artesanías de cerámica y telas hermosas, puedes visitar el estado de

_____ .

2. Los volcanes de Popocatépetl y Ixtaccíhuatl están cerca de la capital, México, D. F., que
también se llama _____ .

3. _____ está cerca de Estados Unidos.

4. El _____, o la Plaza de la Constitución está en el centro histórico de la
Ciudad de México.

5. La ciudad de _____ está al lado de la Bahía de Campeche.

2 México tiene tres volcanes importantes. El primer de ellos es el segundo volcán más
alto de América del Norte y se llama Popocatépetl, o el Popo. El segundo se llama
Ixtaccíhuatl, un nombre azteca que significa **mujer blanca.** El tercero es el volcán
más nuevo del hemisferio occidental y se llama Paricutín. Localízalos y escribe sus
nombres en el mapa.

Map/Culture Activities *México*

3 En las páginas 194 y 195 de tu libro, conoces a algunos mexicanos famosos. Empareja cada persona con la descripción más apropiada.

1. Alfonso Cuarón ____.

2. Laura Esquivel ____.

3. Salma Hayek ____.

4. Frida Kahlo ____.

5. Octavio Paz ____.

6. Diego Rivera ____.

a. Esta persona es escritor y ganó el Premio Nobel de Literatura en 1990.

b. Esta persona fue el director de *Harry Potter y el prisionero de Azkaban*.

c. Esta persona escribió el libro *Como agua para chocolate*.

d. Esta persona es actriz y trabajó en la película *Frida*.

e. Esta persona pintó muchas murales (*murals*) con temas políticos.

f. Esta persona pintó muchos autorretratos (*self-portraits*).

4 En la página 195 hay una foto de la celebración del 15 de septiembre, el Día de la Independencia Mexicana, de la plaza principal de la Ciudad de México. Los mexicanos celebran con fiestas, fuegos artificiales (*fireworks*) y música. ¿Es similar a las celebraciones del 4 de julio donde tú vives?

_____

_____

_____

_____

_____

_____

_____

5 La cultura del estado mexicano de Oaxaca tiene mucha influencia indígena, especialmente de los zapotecas y los mixtecas. ¿Hay mucha influencia indígena donde tú vives? ¿De cuáles grupos nativos es?

_____

_____

_____

_____

_____

_____

_____

Map/Culture Activities Answer Key

MÉXICO

Page 84

Map labels: Baja California, 3, GOLFO DE MÉXICO, GOLFO DE CALIFORNIA, OCÉANO PACIFICO, MÉXICO, 5, BAHÍA DE CAMPECHE, Península de Yucatán, Paricutín, 2, 4, Popocatépetl e Ixtaccíhuatl, Puebla, 1

❶

1.	Oaxaca	**4.**	Zócalo
2.	Ciudad de México	**5.**	Veracruz
3.	Ciudad Juárez		

❷ *Refer to map above.*

Page 85

❸

1.	b	**4.**	f
2.	c	**5.**	a
3.	d	**6.**	e

❹ *Answers will vary.*

❺ *Answers will vary.*

UNIDAD 4

Map/Culture Activities Answer Key

Fine Art Activities

Niña con bandera, Rodolfo Morales

The death of Rodolfo Morales in 2001 was cause for mourning in Mexico. He was known and admired not only for his artwork but also for his involvement in numerous cultural and humanitarian projects, such as the restoration of historic Oaxacan buildings, advocacy for environmental preservation and support of indigenous rights. Morales created a different collage every day, the sale of which benefited his community through the Rodolfo Morales Cultural Foundation. Women, especially indigenous women, figure prominently in most of his paintings. He believed strongly in their vital contribution to Mexican society.

1. Observe the background of the painting. What kind of community do you think the girl belongs to? How can you tell? Use examples from *Niña con bandera* to talk about where the girl lives and what her community is like.

   _____

   _____

   _____

   _____

2. The young girl in this painting is running with the Mexican flag held high in her arms. What do you think Morales was trying to say with this image? Discuss the symbolism of the girl's gesture.

   _____

   _____

   _____

   _____

   _____

   _____

Niña con bandera (1997), Rodolfo Morales. Silkscreen, 65 cm x 50 cm. Courtesy of Galería Arte de Oaxaca, Mexico.

Fine Art Activities

Reina Xochtl, Alfredo Ramos Martínez

Alfredo Ramos Martínez is considered the father of modern Mexican painting. Although he received extensive artistic training, he was inspired by scenes of ordinary life, which led him to abandon the traditional studio setting for the open air of the Mexican marketplace. As the reluctant director of The National Academy in Mexico, Martínez insisted that his students face their subjects in their own environments, as they lived, worked, and played. His focus on nature, the working individual, and the pre-Columbian origins of Mexican society and culture inspired many famous painters for decades to come.

Complete the following activities based on your study of *Reina Xochtl* by Alfredo Ramos Martínez.

1. **a.** Who do you think this woman might be? What features of the painting inform your opinion? Be specific in your answer.

    _____

    _____

    b. Why do you think Martínez refers to this woman as a **reina**, or queen? Do you think the title of the painting is appropriate for the subject? Explore the implications of the painting's title and explain why you do or do not think it is a fitting one.

    _____

    _____

2. Martínez sought to breathe new life into Mexican art by challenging traditional forms and methods. In what ways is this portrait non-traditional? In what ways is it traditional? Use details from *Reina Xochtl* to discuss the ways in which the painting is both conventional and unique.

    _____

    _____

Reina Xochtl, Alfredo Ramos Martínez. Gouache on newspaper. Private Collection/Bonhams, London, UK/Courtesy of Louis Stern Fine Arts, West Hollywood, CA/The Bridgeman Art Library.

Fine Art Activities

La Ciudad de México, Juan O'Gorman

Juan O'Gorman, the son of an Irish father and a Mexican mother, began his career as an architect. His early architectural projects were influenced by the European trends of the time, which emphasized function over form. He later took a break from building design to focus on painting, treating such subject matter as Mexican history, landscapes, and native mythology. Many of his murals and buildings, including banks, schools, and homes, can be seen throughout Mexico. *La Ciudad de México* displays O'Gorman's tendency to incorporate the viewer into his works.

Answer the following questions based on your study of Juan O'Gorman's painting, *La Ciudad de México*.

1. a. What does this painting tell you about the artist's vision of and feelings toward *La Ciudad de México*? Be specific in your answer.

_____

_____

b. How does the artist incorporate the real and the imagined, the literal and the figurative, in his work? Explain the specific images and techniques the artist uses to express both the reality and the essence of *La Ciudad de México*.

_____

_____

_____

2. Describe the builder pictured in the painting. What aspect of Mexican culture and history might he represent? What significance does his presence have in the work? Discuss the figure of the builder and explain your opinion.

_____

_____

_____

Mexico City (1942), Juan O'Gorman. Tempera on masonite. Courtesy of Museo de Arte Moderno, Mexico City, Mexico/Index/© 2005 Sandro Landucci, Mexico City/Estate of Juan O'Gorman/The Bridgeman Art Library.

Fine Art Activities

Plaza Mayor de la Ciudad de México, Anonymous (Mexican School)

Town squares, like the **Plaza Mayor** depicted in this Mexican painting, are capable of revealing many things about a city, from its political and commercial significance, to its social and cultural identity. Mexico's **Plaza Mayor** was a popular subject for colonial artists, who wanted to show the world their sophisticated and elegant city, with its vitality, wealthy citizens, and European architecture.

Study the excerpt of the painting *Plaza Mayor de la Ciudad de México* and complete the following activities.

1. **a.** What types of people are depicted in *Plaza Mayor*? Describe the figures you see in this section of the painting and explain what details the artist used to identify his subjects.

   _____

   _____

   _____

   b. What activities are illustrated? Tell what you think the people are doing.

   _____

   _____

   _____

2. How does this depiction of Mexico City compare with your thoughts or knowledge about what the city is like today? Compare and contrast this vision of the capital with your own.

   _____

   _____

Detail of carriages, *Plaza Mayor in Mexico* (18th century), Mexican School. Oil on canvas. Courtesy of Museo Nacional de Historia, Mexico City, Mexico/Giraudon/The Bridgeman Art Library.

Fine Art Activities Answer Key

NIÑA CON BANDERA, RODOLFO MORALES
Page 87

1. *Answers will vary.* The girl may belong to a traditional rural community. There are few buildings in the background, only a simple house, fields, and mountains beyond.

2. *Answers may vary.* The image seems to reiterate the importance of women in sustaining society; the girl supports the flag, symbolic of the country, etc.

REINA XOCHTL, ALFREDO RAMOS MARTÍNEZ
Page 88

1a. *Answers will vary.* Traditional indigenous women often are featured in Martínez's paintings, and are typically depicted in this pose.

b. *Answers will vary.* The title may point to the importance of the indigenous woman in Mexican society.

2. *Answers will vary.* Like a conventional work, the painting is compositionally balanced in terms of line, color, and movement, while the colors and subject are more non-traditional, and are uniquely Mexican.

LA CIUDAD DE MÉXICO, JUAN O'GORMAN
Page 89

1a. *Answers will vary.* Students may note the artist's affection for his city, illustrated by the "Viva México" banner held by angels.

b. *Answers will vary.* The artist uses realistic images like the map, builder, and cityscape, and incorporates a realistic sense of depth and perspective. The images floating in the sky and the inclusion of the "viewers" hands give the painting a surreal quality.

2. *Answers may vary.* The builder appears to be of indigenous descent, recalling the pre-Columbian history of Mexico, the construction of the modern city on the ruins of the indigenous empire, and the complex role of the indigenous person in Mexican society.

PLAZA MAYOR DE LA CIUDAD DE MÉXICO, ANONYMOUS (MEXICAN SCHOOL)
Page 90

1a. *Answers may vary.* There is a variety of people presented, from clergy to wealthy men and women and street vendors.

b. *Answers may vary.* The carriages of the wealthy pass by as their occupants shop; the vendors sell their products, etc.

2. *Answers will vary.* Students should be able to answer this question without specific knowledge of Mexico, since this is an opinion question, general ideas about the country are sufficient.

Date: _____

Dear Family:

We are about to begin *Unidad 4* of the Level 2 *¡Avancemos!* program. It focuses on authentic culture and real-life communication using Spanish in Mexico. It practices reading, writing, listening, and speaking, and introduces students to culture typical of Mexico.

Through completing the activities, students will employ critical thinking skills as they compare the Spanish language and the culture of Mexico with their own community. They will also connect to other academic subjects, using their knowledge of Spanish to access new information. In this unit, students are learning to narrate past events and activities, ask for and give directions, and describe the following: continuing activities in the past; people, places, and things; early civilizations and their activities; and the layout of a modern city. They are also learning about grammar—past participles as adjectives, the imperfect tense, preterite and imperfect, verbs with i→y spelling change in the preterite, the preterite of **-car, -gar,** and **-zar** verbs, and more verbs with irregular preterite stems.

Please feel free to call me with any questions or concerns you might have as your student practices reading, writing, listening, and speaking in Spanish.

Sincerely,

Family Involvement Activity

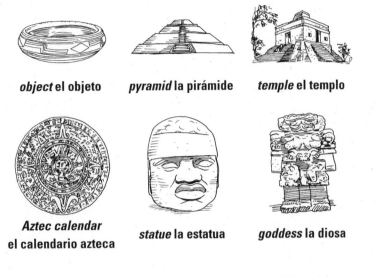

object **el objeto** pyramid **la pirámide** temple **el templo**

Aztec calendar
el calendario azteca statue **la estatua** goddess **la diosa**

STEP 1

With your family, try making a model in dough or clay of each of the objects you see above. Mold the dough or clay with your hands and use toothpicks to help you carve the details. Cut off excess clay or dough with a spatula.

STEP 2

Explain your sculptures to one another. Whenever possible, try to use the Spanish words you have learned in this unit. In the chart, check off the models that you and your family members made out of dough or clay.

Nombre	el objeto	la pirámide	el templo	el calendario azteca	la estatua	la diosa

STEP 3

As you mold the clay, talk with your family members about the legends and myths that you have learned. Try to use Spanish whenever you can.

Absent Student Copymasters

Presentación / Práctica de vocabulario

Materials Checklist

☐ Student text

☐ DVD 2

☐ Video Activities Copymasters, pages 50 and 51

☐ *Cuaderno,* pages 148–150

☐ *Cuaderno para hispanohablantes,* pages 148–151

☐ TXT CD 5 Track 1–2

☐ Did You Get It? Copymasters, pages 1–2

☐ ClassZone.com

Steps to Follow

☐ Read about legends and stories on pages 198 and 199, sections A–F. Look at the pictures to help you understand the text.

☐ Watch the vocabulary video for **Unidad 4**, **Lección 1**. Complete the Video Activities Copymasters.

☐ Read aloud the words in the **Más vocabulario** box on page 198. Say the words aloud two times.

☐ Listen to the CD as you do the **¡A responder!** activity on page 199.

☐ Do **Práctica de vocabulario**, **Actividades 1** and **2** on page 200.

☐ Complete *Cuaderno,* pages 148, 149, and 150.
OR
Complete *Cuaderno para hispanohablantes,* pages 148, 149, 150, and 151.

☐ Check your comprehension by completing the **Para y piensa** box on page 200.

☐ Complete the Did You Get It? Copymasters, pages 1 and 2.

If You Don't Understand . . .

☐ Watch the DVD and listen to the CD in a quiet place. If you get lost, pause and go back as often as necessary.

☐ Read sections A–F on pages 198 and 199 aloud as if you were telling the story.

☐ After you select your answer, read the sentence to check that it makes sense.

☐ If you have a question, write it down to ask your teacher later.

☐ Use the Interactive Flashcards to help you study the lesson.

Absent Student Copymasters

Vocabulario en contexto

Materials Checklist

- ☐ Student text
- ☐ DVD 2
- ☐ Video Activities Copymasters, pages 52 and 53
- ☐ TXT CD 5 Track 3
- ☐ Did You Get It? Copymasters, pages 1 and 3

Steps to Follow

- ☐ Look at the photo on page 201.
- ☐ Read **Cuando lees** and **Cuando escuchas** on page 201.
- ☐ Listen to TXT CD 5 Track 3 as you follow along in the text.
- ☐ Watch the **Unidad 4**, **Lección 1 Telehistoria escena 1** without your text. Then watch the DVD again and complete the Video Activities Copymasters.
- ☐ Complete **Actividades 3** and **4** on page 202. Use the CD with **Actividad 3**.
- ☐ Read the **Nota gramatical** on page 202. Read the sentences aloud in Spanish and in English.
- ☐ Check your comprehension by completing the **Para y piensa** box on page 202.
- ☐ Complete the Did You Get It? Copymasters, pages 1 and 3.

If You Don't Understand . . .

- ☐ Listen to the recordings when you are not distracted by other things. Repeat the sentences you hear on the CD and DVD, and try to copy the pronunciation you hear.
- ☐ Try out the different answers in each sentence. Choose the one that makes the best sense.
- ☐ Read aloud everything that you write. Be sure that you understand what you are reading.
- ☐ If you do not know how to say something, make a note to ask your teacher later.

Absent Student Copymasters

Presentación / Práctica de gramática

Materials Checklist

- [ ] Student text
- [ ] *Cuaderno,* pages 151–153
- [ ] *Cuaderno para hispanohablantes,* pages 152–154
- [ ] TXT CD 5 Track 4–5
- [ ] Did You Get It? Copymasters, pages 4–5, 10
- [ ] ClassZone.com

Steps to Follow

- [ ] Read about the imperfect tense on page 203. Read the conjugation chart aloud a few times.
- [ ] Complete **Actividades 5**, **6**, **7**, and **8** from the text (pp. 204–205). Use TXT CD 5 Track 4 to complete **Actividad 7**.
- [ ] Read the **Comparación cultural** section on page 204. Answer the question in **Compara con tu mundo**.
- [ ] Listen to the **Pronunciación** section on TXT CD 5 Track 5. Pronounce the words aloud. Follow along with it on page 205.
- [ ] Complete *Cuaderno,* pages 151, 152, and 153.
  OR
  Complete *Cuaderno para hispanohablantes,* pages 152, 153, and 154.
- [ ] Check your comprehension by completing the **Para y piensa** box on page 205.
- [ ] Complete the Did You Get It? Copymasters, pages 4, 5, and 10.

If You Don't Understand . . .

- [ ] Listen to the CD in a quiet place and repeat the words you hear aloud.
- [ ] If the directions are unclear, try to restate them in your own words.
- [ ] Read the models several times and substitute other words for the words they use.
- [ ] Follow the model on your paper before trying to write something new yourself.
- [ ] Proofread everything you write for verb-subject agreement and punctuation, and to check that it makes sense.
- [ ] Keep a list of questions and observations to share with your teacher later.
- [ ] Use the Animated Grammar to help you understand.
- [ ] Use the Leveled Grammar Practice on the @Home Tutor.

Absent Student Copymasters

Gramática en contexto

Materials Checklist

☐ Student text

☐ DVD 2

☐ Video Activities Copymasters, pages 54 and 55

☐ TXT CD 5 Track 6

☐ Did You Get It? Copymasters, pages 4, 6, and 11

Steps to Follow

☐ Read **Cuando lees** and **Cuando escuchas** on page 206. Copy the questions.

☐ Listen to TXT CD 5 Track 6 as you read the script of **Telehistoria escena 2**.

☐ Watch the **Unidad 4**, **Lección 1 Telehistoria escena 2** without your text. Then watch the DVD again and complete the Video Activities Copymasters. Try to answer the questions from **Cuando escuchas** as you watch.

☐ Complete **Actividades 9**, **10**, and **11** on page 207. Listen to TXT CD 5 Track 6 or watch the DVD before you complete **Actividad 9**.

☐ Check your comprehension by completing the **Para y piensa** box on page 207.

☐ Complete the Did You Get It? Copymasters, pages 4, 6, and 11.

If You Don't Understand . . .

☐ Watch the DVD where you have no other distractions.

☐ Listen to the CD in a quiet place. If you get lost, pause and go back as often as necessary. Imitate the pronunciation of the voices on the recording.

☐ Follow the style and sentence structure of the model.

☐ Say a few sentences aloud before you choose which one to write down.

☐ Read aloud everything that you write and focus on good pronunciation.

☐ In **Actividad 10**, do the written and verbal parts for both partners.

Absent Student Copymasters

Presentación / Práctica de gramática

Materials Checklist

☐ Student text

☐ *Cuaderno,* pages 154–156

☐ *Cuaderno para hispanohablantes,* pages 155–158

☐ Did You Get It? Copymasters, pages 7, 8, and 12

☐ ClassZone.com

Steps to Follow

☐ Study the review and comparison of the preterite and imperfect tenses presented on page 208.

☐ Complete **Actividades 12**, **13**, **14**, and **15** on pages 209 and 210.

☐ Complete *Cuaderno,* pages 154, 155, and 156.
OR
Complete *Cuaderno para hispanohablantes,* pages 155, 156, 157, and 158.

☐ Check your comprehension by completing the **Para y piensa** box on page 210.

☐ Complete the Did You Get It? Copymasters, pages 7, 8, and 12.

If You Don't Understand . . .

☐ Read the preterite and imperfect lesson several times, both silently and aloud. Make new examples of sentences that use both tenses.

☐ Think about what you are trying to say before you write a sentence. Try several sentences aloud before deciding what to write.

☐ After you write your sentences, read them aloud to make sure they say what you wanted to say.

☐ Read aloud everything that you write. Make sure all the subjects, verbs, and adjectives are in agreement.

☐ If you have any questions, write them down for your teacher.

☐ Use the Animated Grammar to help you understand.

☐ Use the Leveled Grammar Practice on the @Home Tutor.

Absent Student Copymasters

Todo junto

Materials Checklist

- [ ] Student text
- [ ] DVD 2
- [ ] Video Activities Copymasters, pages 56 and 57
- [ ] *Cuaderno,* pages 157–158
- [ ] *Cuaderno para hispanohablantes,* pages 159–160
- [ ] Did You Get It? Copymasters pages 7, 9
- [ ] WB CD 2 Tracks 21–24
- [ ] HL CD 1 Tracks 25–28
- [ ] TXT CD 5 Tracks 7–9

Steps to Follow

- [ ] Look at the photos and read *Strategies* on page 211. Copy the questions.
- [ ] Read the content of **Telehistoria completa (escenas 1–3)** on page 211.
- [ ] Listen to TXT CD 5 Track 7 as you read the script again.
- [ ] Watch the **Unidad 4, Lección 1 Telehistoria completa** without your text. Then watch the DVD again and complete the Video Activities Copymasters.
- [ ] Complete **Actividades 16, 17, 18, 19,** and **20** on pages 212–213. Use TXT CD 5 Tracks 8–9 with **Actividad 19**.
- [ ] Complete *Cuaderno,* pages 157 and 158.
  OR
  Complete *Cuaderno para hispanohablantes,* pages 159 and 160.
- [ ] Check your comprehension by completing the **Para y piensa** on page 213.
- [ ] Complete the Did You Get It? Copymasters, pages 7 and 9.

If You Don't Understand . . .

- [ ] Watch the DVD and listen to the CD in a quiet place where you will not be distracted. Pause and go back if you get lost.
- [ ] Make notes of anything that is still confusing you. Ask your teacher about it later.

Absent Student Copymasters

Lectura y Conexiones

Materials Checklist

☐ Student text

☐ TXT CD 5 Track 10

Steps to Follow

☐ Read **¡Avanza!** and the *Strategy:* **Leer** (p. 214).

☐ Read the feature **Una leyenda mazateca: El fuego y el tlacuache** on pages 214 and 215.

☐ Follow along with the text again as you listen to TXT CD 5 Track 10.

☐ Check your comprehension by completing the **¿Comprendiste?** and **¿Y tú?** sections of the **Para y piensa** box on page 215.

☐ Read **La bandera mexicana** on page 216.

☐ Read **El lenguaje** in **Proyecto 1**. Create new words with the suffix as directed.

☐ Read **Proyecto 2**, **Las ciencias**, and research the city of Tenochtitlán.

☐ Write about the ingredients listed in **Proyecto 3**, **La salud**.

If You Don't Understand . . .

☐ Imitate the pronunciation of the voice on the CD. Listen to the CD at least a couple of times.

☐ Look up words you don't know. Keep a list of new vocabulary.

☐ Write the questions in your notebook before you write your answer.

☐ Keep a list of vocabulary or sentences that you don't understand.

☐ After you write your sentence, proofread it for spelling and verb-subject agreement.

Absent Student Copymasters

Repaso de la lección

Materials Checklist

- [ ] Student text
- [ ] TXT CD 5 Track 11
- [ ] WB CD 2 Tracks 25–30
- [ ] *Cuaderno,* pages 159–170
- [ ] *Cuaderno para hispanohablantes,* pages 161–170

Steps to Follow

- [ ] Read the bullet points under ¡**Llegada!** on page 218.
- [ ] Follow the instructions to complete **Actividades 1**, **2**, **3**, **4**, and **5** (pp. 218–219). Listen to TXT CD 5 Track 11 to complete **Actividad 1**.
- [ ] Complete *Cuaderno,* pages 159, 160, and 161.
- [ ] Complete *Cuaderno,* pages 162, 163, and 164.
  OR
  Complete *Cuaderno para hispanohablantes,* pages 161, 162, 163, and 164.
- [ ] Complete *Cuaderno,* pages 165, 166, and 167.
  OR
  Complete *Cuaderno para hispanohablantes,* pages 165, 166, and 167.
- [ ] Complete *Cuaderno,* pages 168, 169, and 170.
  OR
  Complete *Cuaderno para hispanohablantes,* pages 168, 169, and 170.

If You Don't Understand . . .

- [ ] Read the activity directions two or three times before beginning each activity, at least once silently and once aloud.
- [ ] When there is a model provided in the activity, read it to make sure you understand what you are supposed to do.
- [ ] Underline all of your preterite conjugations. Double underline all imperfect conjugations of verbs.
- [ ] Keep a list of questions for your teacher to answer later.

Absent Student Copymasters

Presentación / Práctica de vocabulario

Materials Checklist

- [ ] Student text
- [ ] DVD 2
- [ ] Video Activities Copymasters, pages 58 and 59
- [ ] *Cuaderno,* pages 171–173
- [ ] *Cuaderno para hispanohablantes,* pages 171–174
- [ ] TXT CD 5 Track 13
- [ ] Did You Get It? Copymasters, pages 13–14
- [ ] ClassZone.com

Steps to Follow

- [ ] Read about ancient civilizations and modern cities on pages 222 and 223, sections A–D. Use the pictures to help you understand the text.

- [ ] Watch the vocabulary video for **Unidad 4, Lección 2.** Complete the Video Activities Copymasters.

- [ ] Read the words in the **Más vocabulario** box on page 223 out loud. Practice using them aloud in sentences.

- [ ] Listen to the CD and do the **¡A responder!** activity on page 223.

- [ ] Do **Práctica de vocabulario, Actividades 1** and **2** on page 224.

- [ ] Complete *Cuaderno,* pages 171, 172, and 173.
  OR
  Complete *Cuaderno para hispanohablantes,* pages 171, 172, 173, and 174.

- [ ] Check your comprehension by completing the **Para y piensa** box on page 224.

- [ ] Complete the Did You Get It? Copymasters, pages 13 and 14.

If You Don't Understand . . .

- [ ] Watch the DVD and listen to the CD as many times as you need to follow the lesson.

- [ ] In **Actividad 1**, look up words you don't understand before choosing the vocabulary word that doesn't fit.

- [ ] In **Actividad 2**, read the descriptions several times before looking at the map.

- [ ] Use the Interactive Flashcards for this lesson to help you practice the vocabulary.

- [ ] If you get confused, write down questions to ask your teacher later.

Absent Student Copymasters

Vocabulario en contexto

Materials Checklist

- [ ] Student text
- [ ] DVD 2
- [ ] Video Activities Copymasters, pages 60 and 61
- [ ] TXT CD 5 Track 14
- [ ] Did You Get It? Copymasters, pages 13 and 15

Steps to Follow

- [ ] Look at the photo and read the **Cuando lees** and **Cuando escuchas** strategies on page 225.

- [ ] Listen to TXT CD Track 14 for **Telehistoria escena 1** as you follow along in the text on p. 225.

- [ ] Watch the **Unidad 4**, **Lección 1 Telehistoria escena 1** without your text. Then watch the DVD again and complete the Video Activities Copymasters.

- [ ] Complete **Actividades 3** and **4** on page 226. Use TXT CD 5 Track 14 with **Actividad 3**.

- [ ] Read the **Nota gramatical** on page 226. Read the conjugations of **leer** and **construir** aloud twice, then spell **leyeron** and **construyeron** with your eyes closed.

- [ ] Check your comprehension by completing the **Para y piensa** box on page 226.

- [ ] Complete the Did You Get It? Copymasters, pages 13 and 15.

If You Don't Understand . . .

- [ ] Pay close attention to the pronunciation in the DVD and CD. If you get lost, pause and go back as often as necessary.

- [ ] Re-read the directions for the activity you find difficult. If you don't understand, try to state them in your own words.

- [ ] Say your sentences aloud before you begin to write. Afterwards, check to make sure that they say what you wanted to say.

- [ ] If you have any questions or doubts, make a list to ask your teacher later.

Absent Student Copymasters

Presentación / Práctica de gramática

Materials Checklist

☐ Student text

☐ *Cuaderno,* pages 174–176

☐ *Cuaderno para hispanohablantes,* pages 175–177

☐ TXT CD 5 Track 15

☐ Did You Get It? Copymasters, pages 16–17, 22

☐ ClassZone.com

Steps to Follow

☐ Read about the preterite of **-car**, **-gar**, and **-zar** verbs on page 227.

☐ Do **Actividades 5**, **6**, **7**, and **8** on pages 228 and 229. Use TXT CD 5 Track 15 with **Actividad 6**.

☐ Read **Comparación cultural** on page 229, then answer the question in **Compara con tu mundo**.

☐ Complete *Cuaderno,* pages 174, 175, and 176.
OR
Complete *Cuaderno para hispanohablantes,* pages 175, 176, and 177.

☐ Check your comprehension by completing the **Para y piensa** box on page 229.

☐ Complete the Did You Get It? Copymasters, pages 16, 17, and 22.

If You Don't Understand . . .

☐ Listen to the CD in a quiet place. If you get lost, pause the CD and go back.

☐ Read the grammar chart on page 227 aloud several times. Practice writing out the spelling changes in the preterite tense before you begin the activities.

☐ Use the models as a guide for your own sentences.

☐ Read aloud everything that you write, and check for spelling and verb-subject agreement as you read.

☐ Keep a list of observations, doubts, and questions to share later with your teacher.

☐ Write and practice the parts of both partners in **Actividad 7**.

☐ Use the Animated Grammar to help you understand.

☐ Use the Leveled Grammar Practice on the @Home Tutor.

Absent Student Copymasters

Gramática en contexto

Materials Checklist

☐ Student text

☐ Video Activities Copymasters, pages 62 and 63

☐ DVD 2

☐ TXT CD 5 Tracks 16–17

☐ Did You Get It? Copymasters, pages 16, 18

Steps to Follow

☐ Look at the **Cuando lees** and **Cuando escuchas** strategies on page 230. Copy the questions.

☐ Listen to TXT CD 5 Track 16 as you read along in the text.

☐ Watch the **Unidad 4**, **Lección 2 Telehistoria escena 2** without your book. Then watch the DVD again and complete the Video Activities Copymasters.

☐ Complete **Actividades 9** and **10** on page 231. Use TXT CD 5 Track 16 with **Actividad 9**.

☐ Listen to TXT CD 5 Track 17 as you read along with **Pronunciación** on page 231.

☐ Check your comprehension by completing the **Para y piensa** box on page 231.

☐ Complete the Did You Get It? Copymasters, pages 16 and 18.

If You Don't Understand . . .

☐ Watch the DVD and listen to the CD where you have no other distractions. If you get lost, pause and go back as necessary.

☐ Say the activity directions in your own words after you read them.

☐ Follow the style and sentence structure of the models.

☐ Think of several ways to state your answer, then choose the best one.

☐ If you have any questions, write them down for your teacher to answer later.

Absent Student Copymasters

UNIDAD 4 Lección 2

Absent Student Copymasters

Presentación / Práctica de gramática

Materials Checklist

☐ Student text

☐ *Cuaderno,* pages 177–179

☐ *Cuaderno para hispanohablantes,* pages 178–181

☐ Did You Get It? Copymasters, pages 19–20, 23

☐ ClassZone.com

Steps to Follow

☐ Read about more verbs with irregular preterite stems on page 232. Read the grammar chart silently and aloud.

☐ Follow the instructions to complete **Actividades 11**, **12**, **13**, and **14** on pages 233 and 234.

☐ Complete *Cuaderno,* pages 177, 178, and 179.
OR
Complete *Cuaderno para hispanohablantes,* pages 178, 179, 180, and 181.

☐ Check your comprehension by completing the **Para y piensa** box on page 234.

☐ Complete the Did You Get It? Copymasters, pages 19, 20, and 23.

If You Don't Understand . . .

☐ Use the models as a guide for your own sentence style and structure.

☐ Read over the directions several times. State them in your own words.

☐ Review everything that you write by reading it aloud. Be sure that you understand what you are reading, and that your answers make sense.

☐ Write irregular verbs on index cards and draw their conjugation charts in the preterite tense on the back.

☐ Use the Animated Grammar to help you understand.

☐ Use the Leveled Grammar Practice on the @Home Tutor.

Absent Student Copymasters
Todo junto

Materials Checklist

☐ Student text

☐ DVD 2

☐ Video Activities Copymasters, pages 64 and 65

☐ *Cuaderno,* pages 180–181

☐ *Cuaderno para hispanohablantes,* pages 182–183

☐ Did You Get It? Copymasters, pages 19, 21

☐ TXT CD 5 Tracks 18–20

☐ WB CD 2 Tracks 31–34

☐ HL CD 1 Tracks 29–32

Steps to Follow

☐ Look at the photos, and read the reading and listening strategies on page 235. Copy the questions.

☐ Listen to TXT CD 5 Track 18 as you read the script of **Telehistoria completa**.

☐ Watch the **Unidad 4**, **Lección 2 Telehistoria completa** without your book. Then watch the DVD again and complete the Video Activities Copymasters.

☐ Complete **Actividades 15**, **16**, and **17** on page 236.

☐ Do **Actividades 18** and **19** on page 237. Listen to TXT CD 5 Tracks 19–20 with **Actividad 18**.

☐ Complete *Cuaderno,* pages 177, 178, and 179.
   OR
   Complete *Cuaderno para hispanohablantes,* pages 178, 179, 180, and 181.

☐ Check your comprehension by completing the **Para y piensa** box on page 237.

☐ Complete the Did You Get It? Copymasters, pages 19 and 21.

If You Don't Understand . . .

☐ Watch the DVD and listen to the CD in a quiet place where you will not be distracted. Pause and go back if you get lost.

☐ Think of several ways to correct the errors. Choose the best one.

☐ Read the models a few times to give you a clear idea of how to complete each activity.

☐ Keep a list of problems you encounter to discuss with your teacher later.

Absent Student Copymasters

Lectura cultural

Materials Checklist

☐ Student text

☐ TXT CD 5 Track 21

Steps to Follow

☐ Read *Strategy:* **Leer** (p. 238).

☐ Read **Los zapotecas y los otavaleños** on pages 238 and 239.

☐ Read the text aloud as you listen to it on TXT CD 5 Track 21.

☐ Check your comprehension by completing the **¿Comprendiste?** and **¿Y tú?** sections of the **Para y piensa** box on page 239.

If You Don't Understand . . .

☐ Listen to the CD in a quiet place. If you get lost, pause the CD and go back.

☐ Reread the text to help you understand the activity questions.

☐ Form your answer before you begin to write anything. Choose the best way to phrase it.

☐ Reread aloud everything that you write. Check for agreement between subjects, verbs, and adjectives.

Absent Student Copymasters

Proyectos culturales

Materials Checklist

☐ Student text

Steps to Follow

☐ Read the text of **Canciones tradicionales de México y Ecuador**, on page 240.

☐ Read the description of **rancheras** in **Proyecto 1**. Read the lyrics to **"Allá en el Rancho Grande."**

☐ Read the lyrics to **"Que Llueva"** in **Proyecto 2**.

☐ Answer the question in the **En tu comunidad** segment.

If You Don't Understand . . .

☐ Ask your family members if they know the tunes to the songs in the lesson.

☐ Read the lyrics silently, then aloud. Sing them if you know the tune.

☐ If you have any questions, write them down so you can ask your teacher later.

☐ Do your work carefully. Write the lyrics to other Spanish language songs you know.

Absent Student Copymasters

Repaso de la lección

Materials Checklist

☐ Student text

☐ TXT CD 5 Track 22

☐ WB CD 2 Tracks 35–40

☐ *Cuaderno,* pages 182–193

☐ *Cuaderno para hispanohablantes,* pages 184–193

Steps to Follow

☐ Read the bullet points under **¡Llegada!** on page 242.

☐ Complete **Actividades 1**, **2**, **3**, and **4** (pp. 242–243). Listen to TXT CD 5 Track 22 to complete **Actividad 1.**

☐ Complete *Cuaderno,* pages 182, 183, and 184.

☐ Complete *Cuaderno,* pages 185, 186, and 187.
OR
Complete *Cuaderno para hispanohablantes,* pages 184, 185, 186, and 187.

☐ Complete *Cuaderno,* pages 188, 189, and 190.
OR
Complete *Cuaderno para hispanohablantes,* pages 188, 189, or 190.

☐ Complete *Cuaderno,* pages 191, 192, and 193.
OR
Complete *Cuaderno para hispanohablantes,* pages 191, 192, and 193.

If You Don't Understand . . .

☐ Repeat aloud with the audio. Try to pronounce words like the people on the recording.

☐ Read the activity directions and study the models when they are given.

☐ Look back through the lesson if you do not remember how to conjugate a verb or how to spell a vocabulary word.

☐ Proofread your work for spelling, punctuation and grammar.

☐ Keep a list of questions for your teacher to answer later.

Absent Student Copymasters

Comparación cultural

Materials Checklist

☐ Student text

☐ *Cuaderno,* pages 194–196

☐ *Cuaderno para hispanohablantes,* pages 194–196

☐ TXT CD 5 Track 23

Steps to Follow

☐ Read the directions in **Lectura y escritura** for **Actividades 1** and **2** on page 244.

☐ Listen to TXT CD 5 Track 23 as you read **Lo antiguo y lo moderno en mi ciudad** in the text on page 245.

☐ Read *Strategy:* **Escribir**, then begin **Actividad 2** (p. 244).

☐ Complete the **Compara con tu mundo** section on page 244.

☐ Complete *Cuaderno,* pages 194, 195, and 196.
OR
Complete *Cuaderno para hispanohablantes,* pages 194, 195, and 196.

If You Don't Understand . . .

☐ Read through the assignment in **Lectura y escritura** before you begin to read the feature so that you understand the activity.

☐ Listen to the recording as many times as you need in order to understand all the speakers.

☐ Keep a list of questions so you can ask your teacher later.

☐ Think about what you want to say before you begin writing. Reread everything you write. Check for punctuation, spelling and verb-subject agreement.

Absent Student Copymasters

Repaso inclusivo

Materials Checklist

☐ Student text

☐ TXT CD 5 Track 24

Steps to Follow

☐ Use the CD to complete **Actividad 1** on page 248.

☐ Complete **Actividades 2**, **3**, **4**, **5**, **6**, and **7** (pp. 248–249).

If You Don't Understand . . .

☐ For **Actividad 1**, listen to the CD in a quiet place. Repeat aloud with the audio.

☐ Read the activity directions silently and aloud. If you don't remember the vocabulary or verb conjugations, go back to the pages in the unit that teach it.

☐ Underline each verb that is conjugated in the preterite tense, and double underline all verbs conjugated in the imperfect tense. Double check them for accuracy.

☐ Write and practice the parts of both partners in all activities that call for partner or group work.

☐ Keep a list of anything that is still difficult for you. Discuss it with your teacher later.